In Praise of the Earth

Byung-Chul Han

In Praise of the Earth
A Journey into the Garden

With illustrations by Isabella Gresser
Translated by Daniel Steuer

polity

Originally published in German as *Lob der Erde. Eine Reise in den Garten* © by Ullstein Buchverlage GmbH, Berlin. Published in 2018 by Ullstein Verlag.

This English translation © Polity Press, 2025.

English translation of Robert Schumann's *Melancholy* (published in *The Book of Lieder* by Faber, 2005) © Richard Stokes.

Polity Press Ltd.
65 Bridge Street
Cambridge CB2 1UR, UK

Polity Press Ltd.
111 River Street
Hoboken, NJ 07030, USA

ISBN-13: 978-1-5095-6789-8 – hardback

A catalogue record for this book is available from the British Library.

Library of Congress Control Number: 2025932451

Typeset in 11pt on 15pt Janson Text
by Cheshire Typesetting Ltd, Cuddington, Cheshire
Printed and bound in Great Britain by CPI Group (UK) Ltd, Croydon

The publisher has used its best endeavours to ensure that the URLs for external websites referred to in this book are correct and active at the time of going to press. However, the publisher has no responsibility for the websites and can make no guarantee that a site will remain live or that the content is or will remain appropriate.

Every effort has been made to trace all copyright holders, but if any have been overlooked the publisher will be pleased to include any necessary credits in any subsequent reprint or edition.

For further information on Polity, visit our website:
politybooks.com

CONTENTS

But ask now the beasts, and they shall teach thee; and the fowls of the air, and they shall tell thee:

Or speak to the earth, and it shall teach thee: and the fishes of the sea shall declare unto thee.

Who knoweth not in all these that the hand of the LORD hath wrought this?

Job 12: 7–9

PREFACE

One day, I suddenly felt a deep longing, even a pressing need, to be close to the earth. Thus, I decided to spend time gardening every day. For three full years, throughout spring, summer, autumn, and winter, I worked in my garden, which I called *Bi-Won* (Korean for 'secret garden'). On the heart-shaped sign that my predecessor had left on a rose arch, it still says 'Dream Garden'. I left the sign in place. My secret garden is, after all, also a dream garden, because there I dream of the *coming earth*.

For me, gardening was a form of silent meditation, a lingering in stillness. It made time *linger and smell*. The longer I kept working in the garden, the more respect I developed for the earth, for its enchanting beauty. I am now deeply convinced that the earth is a divine creation. The garden helped me gain this conviction, helped me gain this insight which for me has become a certainty, has taken on the *character of evidence*. Evidence originally meant *seeing*. I have *seen it*.

The time spent in the flourishing garden has made me devout again. I believe that the *Garden of Eden* has existed and *will exist*. I believe in God, the creator, in this *player* who always begins new games and thereby renews everything. Human beings, as his creation, are obliged *to join in the play*. Labour, or *performance*, destroys the game. It is a blind, blank, dumb doing.

Some of the lines in this book are prayers, confessions, even confessions of love to the earth and nature. There is no biological evolution. Everything is the result of a *divine revolution*. I have *experienced it*. Biology is ultimately a *theology*, a *teaching of God*.

The earth is not a dead, lifeless, mute being but an eloquent living being, a living organism. Even a stone is alive. Cézanne, who was obsessed with Montagne Sainte-Victoire, knew about the secret and the particular *liveliness and vigour of rocks*. Laozi teaches:

The world is a spiritual vessel and cannot be run.
One who runs it destroys it; one who seizes it loses it.[1]

As a spiritual vessel the world is fragile. We today are brutally exploiting it, running it into the ground and destroying it completely.

From the earth emanates the imperative to *spare it* [sie zu *schonen*], that is, *to treat it well* [*sie schön zu behandeln*]. Sparing [*Schonen*] is etymologically related to beauty [mit dem Schönen verwandt]. What is beautiful obliges us, even commands us, to *spare it*. What is *beautiful* must be treated *carefully* [*schonend*]. It is an urgent task, an obligation of humankind, to *spare* the earth because she is beautiful, even *magnificent*.

Sparing calls for praise. The following lines are hymns, hymns of praise to the earth. Like a beautiful *song of the earth*, this *praise of the earth* should ring out. For some, however, it should read like *evil tidings*, in the face of the major natural disasters that are visited upon us today. These disasters are the earth's angry response to human recklessness and violence. We have lost all veneration for the earth. We no longer *see or hear* her.

Oleaceae

Jasminum nudiflorum

Winterreise

I am particularly fond of Franz Schubert's *Winterreise* (Winter journey). The song I have sung most often is 'Dream of Springtime'.

I dreamed of bright flowers
such as blossom in May;
I dreamed of green meadows
and the calling of birds.

And when the cocks crew,
my eyes opened;
it was cold and dark,
on the roof the ravens croaked.

But on the window panes
who had been painting leaves?
Well may you laugh at the dreamer
who saw flowers in winter.[1]

Why would I begin a book on gardens with a reference to winter and *Winterreise?* Does winter not signify the end of time spent in gardens? I neither intend to present my dreams of springtime nor to follow the example of someone like Wilson Bentley (who took 5,000 photographs of snow crystals) and turn my attention to ice flowers.

The Berlin winter is terrible, even devastating. The flames of the inferno would be more endurable than this endless wet and dark coldness. All light seems to have been extinguished.

It is nothing but winter,
winter chill and savage.[2]

When faced with the endless grey of a Berlin winter, there arises – in the depth of winter time – the metaphysical wish for a bright, flowering garden.

Bertolt Brecht's ideal garden, unfortunately, has nothing to say about the cold winter months. It only blossoms from March to October:

By the lake, deep amid fir and silver poplar
Sheltered by wall and hedge, a garden
So wisely plotted with monthly flowers
That it blooms from March until October.[3]

2

Apparently I lack this wisdom of Brecht's gardener, because I have decided to create a garden that blooms throughout the year, from January to December. I prefer metaphysics, the metaphysical desire, to the wisdom of the gardener, his 'letting go'.

Winter Garden

The same metaphysical desire animates Roland Barthes's *Camera Lucida*. It is a book of mourning, a book performing the work of mourning. It invokes Barthes's deceased mother with whom he had lived all his life. The book is based on a photograph which Barthes ceaselessly circles, embraces, even adores, but which is not reproduced in the book. *It shines through its absence.* This photograph shows his mother as a five-year-old girl in a *Winter Garden*.

> Lost in the depths of the Winter Garden, my mother's face is vague, faded. In a first impulse, I exclaimed: 'There she is! She's really there! At last, there she is!'[1]

Barthes distinguishes between two aspects of a photograph: *studium* and *punctum*. *Studium* relates to the information that can be extracted from it, making it possible to study it. The *punctum*, by contrast, does not provide information. Literally it means '*punched point*'; it is derived from the Latin 'pungere' (to stab). The *punctum* affects and shakes the observer.

For me, the *punctum* of *Camera Lucida* is the photograph of the Winter Garden that is not reproduced, with his mother, his only beloved, in it. I now see the Winter Garden double. It is a symbolic place of death and resurrection, a place where the metaphysical work of mourning takes place. *Camera Lucida*, before my eyes, is a flowering garden, a *bright light* within the wintry darkness, life amid death, a celebration of reawakening life amid today's deadly life. A metaphysical light transforms the *chambre noir* into a *chambre claire*, a *bright Winter Garden*.

Roland Barthes loved Romantic song. He took singing lessons. I would have loved to hear him sing. Often I feel that Barthes is singing when writing, or by writing sings. *Camera Lucida* is actually a kind of Romantic cycle of songs with forty-one songs/chapters. Song number twenty-nine is called 'The Little Girl'.

Camera Lucida, to me, sounds like a *Winterreise*, a winter journey. Searching for his mother, his beloved, Barthes travels through the 'realm of the DEAD'. Searching for the *truth* of the mother, he embarks on an endless wandering.

Nor could I omit this from my reflection: that I had discovered this photograph back through Time. The Greeks entered into [the realm of] Death backward: what they had before them was their past. In the same way I worked back through a life, not my own, but the life of someone I love.[2]

5

The 'Winter Garden Photograph', he writes, 'was for me like the last music Schumann wrote before collapsing, that first *Gesang der Frühe* which accords with both my mother's being and my grief at her death'.[3] *Die Gesänge der Frühe* (Songs of dawn), a cycle of five short piano pieces, is Schumann's last piano work. Three days before his attempted suicide, he called them a 'collection of musical pieces which describe the sensations during the approaching and growing morning'. Initially, Clara Schumann did not know how to react to these pieces: 'Very original pieces again, but difficult to comprehend, there is such an altogether peculiar mood in them.'

Die Gesänge der Frühe is suffused with the longing for a newly awakening, resurrected life. These are songs of mourning. A deep melancholy can be heard in them. Death and resurrection are the themes.

When, when will the morning come,
When, O when!
That will free my life
From these bonds?
You my eyes,
So clouded by sorrow!
Saw only torment instead of love,
Saw no joy at all;
Saw only wound on wound,
Agony upon agony inflicted on me;
And in my long life,
Not a single cheerful hour.
If only the hour
Would finally,
Finally arrive,

6

When I could no longer see!
When, when will the morning come,
That will free my life
From these bonds?[4]

A mysterious aura surrounds the first *Gesang der Frühe*. The unfathomable melancholy raises itself up and turns into a delirious state. It is interrupted by elements of restrained jubilation and moments of transfiguration and ecstasy in which the first hesitant glimmers of light break through the darkness.

This moment of early dawn is a 'pre-time' that precedes common time and in which transient time, the time of life and death, is suspended. These *Gesänge der Frühe* invigorate, at-*tune* my imagination of a flowering wintery garden.[5] They provide the fundamental mood of this book.

Ranunculaceae

Flos glacialis

Time of the Other

In the garden, I experience the seasons with much greater intensity than anywhere else. And accordingly, the approaching winter also causes greater suffering. The light gets weaker, thinner, and grows pale. I never used to pay that much attention to the light. Now the dying light causes me pain. In the garden, the seasons are mainly perceived through the body. The icy coldness of the water in the rain barrel enters deep into the body. But the pain I feel from it is soothing, even invigorating. It returns reality, even a corporeality to me that is increasingly lost in today's *well-tempered digital* world. This world does not know of temperature, of pain, of bodies. The garden, however, is richly sensual and material. It is much *richer in world* than a screen.

Since I have begun working in the garden, I experience time differently. It passes much slower. It expands. The time until next spring feels like an eternity. The falling leaves of next autumn lie in an unimaginable distance. Summer too seems infinitely far away. Winter is already lasting forever. Working in the winter garden prolongs it. Never had winter seemed as long as in my first year as a gardener. I suffered a lot from the cold and lasting frost, not because of me, but mostly because of the plants which bloom in winter and kept their flowers despite all the snow and frost. My worry, which was a caring, was mainly about the flowers. The garden moves me one step further away from my ego. I have no children. But through the garden I slowly learn what solicitude, caring for others, means. The garden was a place of love.

The time of the garden is the *time of the other*. The garden has its own time that is proper to it, and not at my disposal. Every plant has its proper time. In the garden, many such proper times overlap. The autumn crocus and the spring crocus look similar, but they have an altogether different *sense of time*. It is astonishing that every plant has a pronounced *temporal awareness*, possibly even more so than humans who, today, somehow seem to be *atemporal, poor in time*. The garden allows an intense experience of time. Through my work in the garden, I have become *rich in time*. The garden for which you work gives much back. It gives me *being and time*. The uncertainty in waiting, the required patience and slow growth create a special feeling for time. In his *Critique of Pure Reason*, Immanuel Kant describes cognition as a process of acquiring something. Cognition, he says, aims at 'a really new acquisition [Erwerb]'.[1] In the first edition of *Critique of Pure Reason*, he spoke of 'cultivation' [Anbau] instead of 'acquisition'.[2]

10

What might have motivated Kant to replace 'cultivation' with 'acquisition' in the second edition?

Maybe 'cultivation' reminded Kant too much of the dangerous power of the elements, of the *earth* and the uncertainty that is immanent to it, of the resistance and power of nature that would have severely disturbed the Kantian subject's feeling of autonomy and freedom. Urban employees can acquire what they need through work that is independent of the changing seasons, something not possible for a farmer who must follow the seasons' rhythm. Waiting, or patience, which Kant denigrates as a 'feminine virtue', but which one needs to show with regard to the slow growth of what is entrusted to the earth, may well be alien to the Kantian subject. The uncertainty to which the farmer is exposed may be intolerable for a Kantian subject.[3]

In 'Love and Knowledge', Max Scheler mentions that

Augustine speaks in mysterious ways, for example, of the tendency of plants, when looked at by humans, to be 'redeemed' in this viewing from their particular existence of being closed into themselves. It is as though what happens to plants through knowledge derived from love is a kind of analogue to the redemption that leads people back to God through Christ.[4]

Knowledge is not acquisition, not *my* acquisition, not *my* redemption, but redemption of the *other*. Knowledge is love. The loving gaze, knowledge guided by love, redeems the flower from its lack of being. The garden, thus, is a *place of redemption*.

Adoxaceae

Viburnum bodnantense

Back to the Earth

*We called the earth one of the flowers of heaven, and heaven
we called the infinite garden of life.*

Friedrich Hölderlin, *Hyperion*[1]

Adorno offers a philosophical explanation for the passion
I harbour for Schubert. 'Schubert's music brings tears
to our eyes, without first consulting the soul.'[2] Thus, we
cry without knowing: *why?* Schubert's music disarms the
'subject of action'. It rattles the ego and triggers a so to
speak pre-reflective, reflex-like crying.

Dissolved in tears, the ego gives up its superiority and
becomes aware that it is part of nature. In crying it returns
to the earth. For Adorno, the earth is the antipode to the
subject that posits itself as something absolute. The earth
liberates the subject from being captivated within itself.

Recollection of nature breaks the arrogance of his self-positing: 'My tears well up; earth, I am returning to you.' With that, the self exits, spiritually, from its imprisonment in itself.[3]

The digitalization of the world, which amounts to its complete anthropomorphizing, to turning it into something subjective, makes the earth disappear altogether. We cover it over with our own retina and thereby become blind for the other.

The more densely people have spun a categorial web around what is other than subjective spirit, the more fundamentally have they disaccustomed themselves to the wonder of that other and deceived themselves with a growing familiarity with what is foreign.[4]

The French for 'digital' is 'numérique'. The numerical demystifies, de-poeticizes, de-romanticizes the world. It deprives it of all secrets, of all foreignness, and transforms everything into the well-known, banal, into the familiar, the 'Like', into the same. Everything becomes *commensurable*. In the face of the world's digitalization, the task would be to *re-romanticize* it, to rediscover its poetic nature, to give it back the dignity of the mysterious, of beauty, and of the sublime.

For the first time in my life I dug in the soil. With my spade I went deep into the ground. The grey, sandy earth that came up was alien to me, seemed almost uncanny. I was astonished by its mysterious heaviness. While digging I came across many roots which, however, I could not attribute to any plant, any nearby tree. Thus, there was a secret *life* down there, which up until then had been unknown to me.

Berlin has a very special soil. It developed through the sedimentation of sand during the Ice Age. Such soils are found on outwash plains, also called sandur or Geest. The name Geest goes back to the Low German adjective 'güst', meaning 'dry' or 'infertile'.

Berlin is located in a glacial valley that was formed about 8,000 years ago at the end of the last Ice Age, the so-called Weichselian glaciation. The valley acted as a drainage channel for the water from melted inland glaciers during the time of the Frankfurt phase when the limit of glaciation lay at Frankfurt/Oder. Its formation coincided with that of the Baruth glacial valley further south, and it was the drainage channel towards the North Sea.

When you delve deeper into the earth's history, you begin to feel a deep reverence for the earth, which today, unfortunately, is exposed to total exploitation. The earth is literally disfigured. We should learn again to wonder at the earth, at her beauty and strangeness, her uniqueness. In the garden I experience that the earth is magical, enigmatic, and mysterious. As soon as you treat her as a resource to be exploited you have already destroyed her.

The St.-Matthäus-Kirchhof cemetery in Schöneberg is situated on an elevation. Großgörschenstraße, the street leading to it, rises slightly at this point because the melting ice formed a slope. The cemetery lies on this slope. The Brothers Grimm and Immanuel Hegel, one of Hegel's sons, are buried here. The peak of the slope is Schöneberg's highest point above sea level. In prehistoric times, glacial water ran down the slightly sloping Langenscheidtstraße nearby.

I often touch the earth with amazement and stroke it. For me, every shoot that comes out of the earth is a genuine miracle. It is astounding that in the middle of a cold and dark universe there is a place of life like the earth. We should always keep in mind that we are living on a small but prospering planet in an otherwise lifeless universe, that we are planetary beings. What is required is a *planetary consciousness*. It is regrettable that the earth is exploited with such brutality. The planet is almost bleeding to death. Drugged child soldiers are used in bloody wars over the so-called rare-earth elements. We have lost all sensitivity for the earth. We no longer know what the earth is. We take it solely as a resource which, at best, one should treat in a sustainable manner. To *spare* the earth means to give it back its essence. Thus, Heidegger writes about saving the earth:

> Mortals dwell in that they save the earth – taking the word in the old sense still known to Lessing. Saving does not only snatch something from a danger. To save really means to set something free into its own presencing. To save the earth is more than to exploit it or even wear it out. Saving the earth does not master the earth and does not subjugate it, which is merely one step from spoliation.
>
> Mortals dwell in that they receive the sky as sky. They leave to the sun and the moon their journey, to the stars their courses, to the seasons their blessing and their inclemency; they do not turn night into day nor day into a harassed unrest.[5]

Since I began to work in the garden, I am carrying a strange feeling with me wherever I go, a feeling that was previously unknown to me and that is also intensely physical. It is probably a *feeling of earth* that makes me happy. Maybe the earth is a synonym for the kind of happiness that, today, moves further and further away from us. *Back to the earth* would then mean *back to happiness*. The earth is the source of happiness. We are leaving the earth behind, not least in the wake of the digitalization of the world. We no longer receive the invigorating, exhilarating force of the earth. The earth is reduced to the size of a screen.

For Novalis, the earth is a place of redemption and bliss. In his novel *Henry of Ofterdingen*, an old miner sings a beautiful *song of the earth*:

Who fathoms her recesses,
Is monarch of the sphere, –
Forgetting all distresses,
Within her bosom here.

. . .

He is unto her plighted,
And tenderly allied, –
Becomes by her delighted,
As if she were his bride.[6]

Ranunculaceae

Hepatica nobilis

Romanticizing the World

Novalis defines Romanticism as follows:

> By endowing the commonplace with a higher meaning,
> the ordinary with mysterious respect, the known with
> the dignity of the unknown, the finite with the appear-
> ance of the infinite, I am making it Romantic.[1]

The garden in winter is a Romantic place. There is something mysterious, magical, fairy-tale-like about every sign
of flowering life in the midst of winter. The wintry garden
in bloom preserves the *romantic appearance of the infinite*.

The blue flower is the central symbol of Romanticism.
It stands for love and longing, and embodies the metaphysical desire for the infinite. There is a dream scene in
Novalis's *Henry of Ofterdingen* in which the blue flower
appears to the protagonist:

A sweeter slumber now overcame him. He dreamed of many strange events, and a new vision appeared to him. He dreamed that he was sitting on the soft turf by the margin of a fountain whose waters flowed into the air, and seemed to vanish in it. Dark blue rocks with various colored veins rose in the distance. The daylight around him was milder and clearer than usual; the sky was of a sombre blue, and free from clouds. But what most attracted his notice, was a tall, light-blue flower, which stood nearest the fountain, and touched it with its broad, glossy leaves. Around it grew numberless flowers of varied hue, filling the air with the richest perfume. Be he saw the blue flower alone, and gazed upon it with inexpressible tenderness. He at length was about to approach it, when it began to move, and change its form. The leaves increased their beauty, adorning the growing stem. The flower bended towards him, and revealed among its leaves a blue, outspread collar, within which hovered a tender face.[2]

A garden full of blue flowers – that would be very romantic. The blue flower's model is said to have been the heliotrope, *Heliotropium arborescens*. It is also called Peruvian Turnsole and has a fine scent of vanilla. Thus, in German yet another name for it is 'Vanilleblume', vanilla flower. In my garden, Novalis's romantic flower grows next to cornflowers and flax, both also blue flowers.

The poem *Die blaue Blume* [The blue flower] is by Joseph von Eichendorff. Within the Romantic Movement, the motif of the blue flower became the symbol for eternal longing and wandering in search of happiness:

I search for the blue flower
I search and never have seen it,
A dream tells me of that flower
And my happiness flow'ring within it.

I am wand'ring with my harp
Through countries, cities and leas,
To see whether anywhere
The blue flower appears.

I have been wand'ring for a long time,
A long time have hoped, trustfully relied,
But alas, nowhere yet has
The blue flower come into sight.[3]

According to Goethe's *Theory of Colours*, blue, as opposed to yellow, contains an element of darkness. Blue 'has a peculiar almost indescribable effect on the eye'. Blue, 'in its highest purity is, as it were, an enticing nothingness [reizendes Nichts]'.[4] A wonderful expression: *an enticing nothingness*. Romanticism itself is such an enticing nothingness. The appearance of blue is 'a kind of contradiction between excitement and repose'. First of all, blue is a colour of distance. This is why I love this colour of Romanticism. It awakens a longing:

780. As the upper sky and distant mountains appear blue, so a blue surface seems to retire from us.
781. But as we readily follow an agreeable object that flies from us, so we love to contemplate blue, not because it advances to us, but because it draws us after it.[5]

21

Blue is the colour of seduction, of desire, and of longing. It is opposed to yellow. I do not really like yellow because it is 'the colour nearest the light'.[6] I am a night person. I avoid the bright, glaring light. I feel secure in the night's darkness. Thus, I sleep throughout all of the morning. I prefer bright shadows over sunlight. The appearance of yellow, for me, is too cheerful and carefree. It is not my colour, but I give it a lot of space in my wintry garden because many winter bloomers have yellow flowers, such as winter aconite and winter jasmine. No other colour is able to bring as much light into the winter as yellow. Thus, it is also a colour of hope.

Winter-flowering Cherry

With yellow pears the land
And full of wild roses
Hangs down into the lake,
You lovely swans,
And drunk with kisses
You dip your heads
Into the hallowed, the sober water

But oh, where shall I find
When winter comes, the flowers, and where
The sunshine
And shade of the earth?
The walls loom
Speechless and cold, in the wind
Weathercocks clatter.

Friedrich Hölderlin, *The Middle of Life*[1]

Rosacceae

Prunus subhirtella

In Goethe's *The Sorrows of Young Werther*, there is a madman who is looking for flowers in winter to give to his beloved:

Unfortunate being! And yet I envy your fate: I envy the delusion to which you are a victim. You go forth with joy to gather flowers for your princess, – in winter, – and grieve when you can find none, and cannot understand why they do not grow.[2]

Flowers in winter, one might think, are the stuff of dreams and delusions. But you do not have to be dreaming in order to see flowers in winter, because there are quite a lot of plants which prefer to bloom in winter. Some winter bloomers can even withstand frost over long periods of time. Numerous winter bloomers even blossom in snow. That is very comforting.

I began gardening in the summer, and from the very beginning my work aimed at making the garden bloom in winter. I was almost obsessed with this idea, even intoxicated by it. My ambition was to bring together in my garden each and every winter bloomer.

Before describing winter bloomers, I would like to mention daisies. When they began to flower in the grass, I took great joy in them. I found them beautiful because they were so simple and unassuming. But soon I discovered that they push out the grass and proliferate rampantly. Thus, I declared them to be weeds and tried all sorts of means to get them out of the lawn. I even resorted to chemicals, weed killers. But now, in the winter, I have taken to the daisies again, and I have apologized for my misdeeds, because they keep flowering boldly into the winter. They defy the life-threatening cold. This long-lasting period of flowering might have given them their beautiful botanical name, *Bellis perennis*, the lasting beauty. It is probably a flower that possesses metaphysical desire, a true Platonic plant. Some of them keep flowering steadfastly in the winter frost. Next spring and summer I shall not be belligerent towards them and shall happily let them thrive on the lawn, so that they can again fearlessly defy the winter. The lasting beauty should feel comfortable in my garden. And weeds grow apace.³ *Bellis perennis*, thus, is an image of imperishability.

When after the first frost the garden began to look desolate, I was pleasantly surprised by winter jasmine (*Jasminum nudiflorum*). In the winter cold, it flowered in bright yellow. Its beautifully deep green branches gave the wintry garden a spring-like atmosphere. Winter jasmine resembles forsythia. But whereas the forsythia's flower is made up of four petals, that of winter jasmine has five or six. Winter jasmine is a real miracle. In the middle of winter it conjures up spring. What is enticing about winter jasmine is that its flowers open up only gradually. For me it is the flower of hope par excellence. Across an extended period of time it made sure that my winter garden was in bloom.

Winter jasmine was introduced into Europe from China only as late as 1844. Goethe's *The Sorrows of Young Werther* was published in 1774. The madman of the novel thus had no chance of finding the bright yellow winter flower. I would have loved to give him a flowering branch of winter jasmine as a present so that he could have delighted his beloved.

26

A special winter bloomer is the winter cherry (*Prunus subhirtella autumnalis*). It is a cherry, but prefers to flower in winter instead of spring. Thus, in German it is also called Schneekirsche, snow cherry. It blossoms as early as December. My cherry festival begins in deep winter.

In early January, the dreaded persisting frost arrived. Temperatures plummeted to minus ten degrees. The frost lasted for more than two weeks. There was also a lot of snowfall. Against my expectation, the winter jasmine could not withstand the persisting frost. Its bright yellow flowers withered. Winter cherry and the winterflowering fragrant viburnum, which had blossomed very early because of the mild winter, could also not cope with the frost. Their flowers turned brown and mushy. In the end, it was the winter aconites, snowdrops, winter heath, and witch hazel that sturdily kept their shape and colour despite snow and lasting frost. They made sure that there was not a single day without a blossom in my wintry garden. Even during the deepest winter, my garden was in bloom.

Ranunculaceae

Eranthis hyemalis

Winter Aconites and Witch Hazel

In winter too there are scents. Winter is not a fragrance-free desert. A garden centre provides the following classification for smells in winter:

In the garden: snowdrops, winter aconites, winter-flowering fragrant viburnum, and witch hazel. On fields and in nature: snow and shrubs. On farms: silage, hay, cows, horses, and slaughtering.[1]

Because I do not particularly like animal smells and meat, the only candidates for winter smells for me are the smell of plants and snow. But how does snow smell? Even if I was deaf and blind, I would, on an early winter morning, at once notice when a lot of snow had fallen overnight. The smell of snow is as unimposing, as subtle as the scent of time, as the scent of the awakening morning, and so only few people are able to notice it.

There are far more winter plants that are fragrant than just winter aconite, fragrant viburnum, and witch hazel. The winter-flowering honeysuckle (*Lonicera fragrantissima*), for instance, smells wonderfully like lemon. Wintersweet (*Chimonanthus praecox*), by contrast, smells intensely like musk.

The German for winter aconite is Winterling, a very beautiful name. Its Latin name is *Eranthis hyemalis*. As early as the sixteenth century, the botanist Joachim Camerarius the Younger brought it from Italy to Germany and cultivated it in his garden in Nuremberg. Winter aconites are snow bloomers. *Hyemalis* means 'wintry'. *Eranthis* is made up of the Greek words *éar*, for 'spring', and *anthe*, for blossom. Winter aconites blossom from February to March. In my garden, the plants began to sprout already at the end of December. They look very funny. The almost cheerful yellow blossoms shine above deep green leaves which form a collar. On warm and sunny winter days, the plants attract the first bees. As early as May, their leaves turn yellow. And in June winter aconites retreat fully into the earth for a long summer sleep. They have beautiful star-shaped seed capsules which look like a blossom. Apparently, winter aconites abhor the summer. For me, they are kindred spirits. I too prefer coldness over heat. If I were a flower, I would like to blossom in the middle of winter.

You buy aconites as small bulbs that look like pebbles. I asked myself: how can life grow out of this dead thing? In the garden centre, they are offered in bags. Only later I learned that these desiccated bulbs would never sprout. Thus, I got fresh ones from a flower bulb merchant. They looked very different and already showed white buds. Another merchant, who specializes in winter aconites, even only offers them already planted in pots.

In Germany, the only commonly known winter aconite is the Southern European species with yellow flowers. The Turkish species *Eranthis cilicica* does not differ essentially from it. It just flowers a little later than *Eranthis hyemalis*. But there are many more kinds of winter aconites. *Eranthis Lady Lamortagne* produces double-flowers. *Eranthis Schlyters Triumph* has an orange-yellow blossom. I have both kinds in my garden. I would also like to have winter aconites with white blossoms. *Eranthis pinnatifida* is from Japan and has white blossoms. The white-flowering winter aconite from North Korea, *Eranthis stellate*, is also a beautiful sight to behold. These species have more grace than *Eranthis hyemalis*. I asked a specialist in winter bloomers near Potsdam whether he knew the white-flowering winter aconites. He said yes, and that several times he had tried to cultivate them. But he had failed because of the different climatic conditions in Germany. Far East winters are very dry. The white-flowering winter aconites do not tolerate the cold wetness of a Berlin winter. This year, the Berlin-based bulb merchant Albrecht Hoch, a business that goes back to 1893, offered white-flowering winter aconites from Japan. I immediately ordered some bulbs. Hopefully, they will blossom on the warmer days of next winter.

Many winter bloomers are similar in character. Almost all of them are poisonous, not only winter aconites but also crocuses, Christmas rose, and snowdrops. I like in particular the character of the Christmas rose. Like me, it does not like to travel. You need to leave it where it is. Replanting is poison for it. It does not want to be disturbed.

Like winter aconites and witch hazel, snowdrops are proper winter bloomers. They easily survive snow and temperatures far below zero. There are different varieties. Some of them look truly charming. In my garden, I have a snowdrop with orange-coloured stripes. Snowdrops dream in the middle of winter, their tiny heads pensively bowed.

Another German name for snowdrops is Hübsches Februar-Mädchen – the pretty maiden of February. Their bowed heads give an impression of shyness. For me, snowdrops are not messengers of spring. Rather, they are awakening life in the middle of winter. They have a much more sublime appearance than winter aconites. Their ability to maintain colour and shape even under conditions of snow and frost is impressive.

The witch hazel deserves a special mention. It is a genuine winter bloomer that is well adapted to the winter and temperatures below freezing. As the name suggests, there is something magical about these shrubs.[2] They seem to be enchanted. As early as December, they begin to bloom. I planted two witch hazels in the autumn. They have red flowers. Later, I added a yellow-flowering witch hazel. A wonderful scent radiates from it. The witch hazel that is sold in Germany is a hybrid of the Japanese and Chinese varieties. Interestingly, many shrubs that bloom in winter are from the Far East. Metaphysical desire is in general alien to Asians. Why then do they bloom at that time of year which is hostile to life?

The blossoms of the witch hazel look very peculiar, almost droll. They consist of curled threads. When the temperature drops below zero, the threads roll up. When it gets warmer, they unfurl again. The botanical name of the witch hazel is *Hamamelis*. *Hama* means 'together' and *melon* means 'fruiting'. The name derives from the fact that two fruits ripen in one capsule. Thus, they represent a love couple. It is probably love that makes them blossom in the season that is hostile to life. This makes the witch hazel the flower of faithfulness.

Some plants are surrounded by legends and myths. The mandrake whose roots resemble the human form, for example, is said to have magic powers. According to folk-lore, the deafening noise when its root is pulled out causes death. They are very delicate plants. I have planted several mandrakes in my garden. But they did not thrive and they all died. It seems that my garden loves *stillness*.

I should not forget to say something about liverwort. I bought them from the same gardener from whom I got the winter aconites and pheasant's eyes. As far as liverwort is concerned, this gardener is a true master – he wrote a voluminous encyclopaedia about them. The liverwort is one of the most beautiful flowers in my garden. Every now and again, it produces a bright blue blossom in the middle of winter. For me, it is the *Blue Flower* par excellence. The plant looks very fragile and somehow as if receding. I love its noble weakness. It only carries a few graceful liver-shaped leaves.

White Forsythia

I have a special affection for white forsythia (*Abeliophyllum distichum*). It comes from my homeland, South Korea. It is an endemic plant, that is, a plant growing only within a clearly delimited territory. It only flourishes in seven habitats in mid-South Korea. I found it, however, in a Berlin nursery. Its blossom is snow white and has a very fine almond scent.

Its Korean name is *Misonnamu*. The Korean habitats are protected as natural monuments. *Namu* is Korean for tree. *Mison* was originally the name of a traditional Korean fan. White forsythias are called *Mison* because their fruits have the shape of a fan. *Misonnamu* – it is a very beautiful name. If I had a son, I would name him *Namu*. If I had a daughter, I would give her the name *Mison* or *Nabi* (butterfly).

Hamamelidaceae

Hamamelis

Nabi: Why is there something at all, rather than nothing? The tree . . . the butterfly . . .
Namu: The butterfly is there, so that the tree does not
feel lonely.
Nabi: And the tree?
Namu: So that the butterfly can rest after fluttering
around.

Of course, deep in winter one cannot expect a lavish
summerly display of flowers. Winter only brings forth
delicate, tender, fragile forms. In *Walden*, Henry David
Thoreau writes:

Many of the phenomena of Winter are suggestive of an
inexpressible tenderness and fragile delicacy.[1]

All winter bloomers are somehow very fragile, delicate,
and tender. However, because of their reserved nature
they have an extremely noble appearance. This is why I
love them.

When the time of severe and persisting frost is over,
my wintry garden conjures up a little spring-time in the
middle of winter. At the beginning of February 2016, the
winter aconites were in full bloom. They were a pleasure
to behold. And all around there were snowdrops. They
seemed sad, with their bowed heads. They might as well
have been called *mourning drops*. Especially in snow, they
look enticing. They seem to love the wintry cold. And the
witch hazel reliably continued to bloom. It spirits away
the winter.

The daisies also simply ignore the winter. Being con-
tinuously present, they truly live up to their name: *Bellis*

perennis. The winter heath sturdily continues to flower in early February, as if simply not paying any attention to the winter. Also worth mentioning is the early alpine rose (*Rhododendron praecox*), which produces its delicate red blossoms in early February.

Anemones

In the middle of winter, on a still cold February day, I was very surprised by a small blue flower. I suddenly saw something bright blue in the wintry flower bed. It was an early flowering Balkan anemone, *Anemone blanda*, also called Grecian or winter windflower. It flowers even earlier than crocuses. I was so surprised because until then I only had Japanese anemones in my garden, and they flower in autumn. In German, the early flowering anemone is called 'Strahlenanemone', radiant anemone, because of its appearance. And, indeed, its bright purple-blue flowers shine in the winter cold. It ventures into the daylight as soon as the first rays of sun begin to melt the covering of snow. For me, alongside winter aconites and snowdrops, the radiant Balkan anemone clearly counts as a winter bloomer.

Only now do I understand Gottfried Benn's poem *Anemone*:

Sublime mover – : Anemone,
the earth is cold, is nothing,
your crown alone murmurs
a word of hope, of light.

Into a world without mercy
which only power directs,
your gentle blooms
are sown in silence.

Sublime mover – : Anemone,
bearer of faith, of light,
which one day, from heavy blossom,
the summer will weave into a crown.[1]

When I first read this poem while studying German as a minor subject, I did not even know what an anemone looked like. Nevertheless, I liked the poem because of its remarkable emotional expressiveness. Once I noticed that flowers frequently feature in German poems, I felt the need to buy an encyclopaedia of flowers, so that I could look up any flower that came up and was unknown to me. I wanted to know at least what they looked like.

On the day in February I mentioned, the earth was indeed still cold. And then this small blue flower sprouted out of the ground. It really was a sublime mover. The blue anemone as an expression of faith, of light, stood up against the wintry nothingness. Despite its delicate appearance, there is something heroic about it. As opposed to Gottfried Benn, I would, however, not deny the world, the earth, all mercy. Not only is the earth merciful, but also generous and hospitable. After all, even in the middle of winter it produces wonderfully flowering life.

Camellias

I have planted some camellias in my garden. They are also winter bloomers. In a mild winter, they blossom in mid-February. Last year's winter was very cold. At times, temperatures dropped below minus fifteen degrees. I protected the camellias by wrapping them in fleece. And yet the frost nearly killed them. The Berlin climate is simply not suitable for them. Their flower buds, however, survived, although they blossomed only in late spring. The white flowers were all the more beautiful for the fact that they had survived the deadly winter. Their flowering delighted me. Flowering is rapture. This year, I again wrapped the camellias in a blanket to keep them warm. I protect them. They are my special fosterlings.

In the south east of South Korea, in Busan, home to the best-known film festival in the Far East, there is an island called Camellia Island. The film festival takes place nearby. I enjoyed visiting the island. It is full of camellia trees. The climate in Busan is fairly mild. Thus, they flower gloriously in mid-winter at the seaside.

Theaceae

Camellia japonica

Willow Catkins

Oh, it was with heavenly anticipation I now greeted the coming spring! As from afar on a silent breeze the sounds of the loved one's lyre when all are sleeping, so spring's soft melodies wafted round my breast, as if from Elysium I sensed its coming when the dead branches stirred and a gentle breath caressed my cheek.

Friedrich Hölderlin, *Hyperion*[1]

To me, springtime announces itself acoustically. As early as February, the cooing of the doves suddenly takes on a different timbre. Thus, I first *hear* the approaching spring. So it was this year too. Spring began with a sound.

Spring has arrived after all – incredible! In deep winter, it had been *outside time* for me, *even outside the possible*. It had been pushed into a far distance. While working in the winter garden, spring had seemed *impossible* to me.

If winter means a season without flowering, then I did not have a winter this year. Even under conditions of persistent frost, there had always been a blossom, some flowering life. My wintry garden transformed winter into a spring. The proper spring is therefore another spring, a second, a late spring, a *lateling*.

In 2016, the first warm spring day was 28 March. On this day – I had slept little the previous night – I felt almost dizzy because of the sprouts shooting up everywhere. I noticed a real ecstasy among the plants which was transferred to me. At the same time, it was mixed with timid hesitation. I was a little dazed, intoxicated by the newly awakening life. Thus, I can understand Hyperion very well when he says:

We remembered the past May, we'd never before seen the earth as then, we said, it had been transformed, a silver cloud of blossom, a joyful flame of life, freed of all coarser stuff.

'Oh! all was so full of joy and hope,' cried Diotima, 'so full of ceaseless growth and yet so effortless too, so blissfully at peace, like a child lost in play with not a thought in the world.'

'It's by this that I know it, the soul of nature,' I cried, 'by this still fire, by this lingering in its mighty haste.'[2]

In springtime, there is an awakening of new life spreading out of branches that look completely dead. From dead stumps, fresh green sprouts shoot forth. I wonder why humans are denied the ability to perform this astonishing miracle. They age and die. For them, there is no spring, no reawakening. They wither and decompose. They are condemned to this sad, actually unbearable fate. This makes me envy plants very much; they keep regenerating, gaining new life, rejuvenating. There is always a new beginning. Why is this denied to humans?

Hyperion also laments this fact:

All things age and renew themselves. Why are we excluded from nature's beautiful cycle? Or does it hold for us too?[3]

If the wonderful cycle of nature would also apply to us, we too would be capable of a new beginning, of a mysterious rejuvenation, a resurrection. Why do we have to become weaker and weaker, continue ageing until we disappear for good, without any possibility of a return to life? Why?

The Christmas rose, for example, is practically immortal as long as you leave it alone. They do not like to be moved or to travel. Maybe mortality is the bitter price we have to pay for having separated from the earth, for being able to move around freely, for being independent, free-*standing* selves. Freedom, then, is probably mortality.

The ecstasy of spring truly began with the willow catkins. Up until then, I did not know what becomes of them. I knew them as buds that feel velvety and are offered in flower shops in the spring. I did not even know that they are buds. I was in some way indifferent not only towards willow catkins but towards all plants. Today I see my former indifference as an embarrassing blindness, maybe even as a sin.

On a very warm spring day, all of the willow catkins in my garden flowered at once. They exploded (there is no other word for it). Each of the catkins brought forth innumerable small single flowers with bright yellow pollen. Thus, each transformed into a bright yellow floral cluster. The willow seemed to indulge in ecstasy. It attracted a large swarm of bees. I wondered where the bees came from. A moment ago, it had been cold winter. It felt as if they turned up out of nowhere. As if inebriated, they wallowed in the sea of pollen. In the shortest of times, the willow was emptied. I had never seen anything like it before. I was amazed by this wonderful natural phenomenon.

Crocuses

When spring is approaching, I like to sing Robert Schumann's *A Poet's Love*. There is probably no other song that fits spring better than the cycle's first song:

'Twas in the beauteous month of May,
When all the flowers were springing,
That first within my bosom
I heard love's echo ringing.[1]

My favourite time for singing this song is a warm March day. May, for me, is already too summer-like. The word 'May', incidentally, is derived from the Italian God of growth. 'Growth' [Wachstum] is not really a nice word. We can hear the sound of 'ushering' [Wuchern] in it.[2] Spring, however, is *shy, reserved*.

When I have not seen my garden for several days, I miss it like a beloved. Thus, spring is a special time for me. Love blossoms. In springtime, my love for my garden is particularly strong.

When I did not yet have a garden, I often went to the St.-Matthäus-Kirchhof in Berlin-Schöneberg in order to admire the first crocuses. One almost has to catch them red-handed, so to speak, the very moment they begin to bloom. On a warm winter or early spring day they suddenly shoot out of the ground and open their buds. They make me very happy. This year, I discovered two early bloomers already at the end of February, probably the first ones. It gave me great joy.

I planted many crocuses in my garden. When they begin to bloom in springtime, the garden takes on a fairytale atmosphere. When it is still winter, crocuses very reliably announce the coming of spring. This year, I will plant *Crocus imperati*. In German it is called Teufels-Krokus (devil's crocus); as far as resistance to the cold is concerned it beats all other crocuses. Even minus fifteen degrees cannot do it any harm. It truly is a winter crocus. Thus, it will be the *silently blooming emperor* of my winter garden.

Plantain Lilies (Hosta)

When I took over the garden, two plantain lilies were standing in the shaded part at the back. At first, I did not pay any attention to them. I did not find them particularly beautiful and did not see any nobleness or beauty in them. At first impression, there was something crude, even vulgar about them. Compared to the lush leaves, their blossoms were rather unassuming. I saw nothing but richly proliferating green in them. Their large leaves, coloured green or in shades of yellow, looked rough, even coarse, to me.

Today, I am embarrassed about my initial judgement, about my condemnation of the plantain lilies. It was wrong and unjust. It was based on my ignorance. I was simply blind to the beauty of the plantain lilies. Now, I happily take back my judgement. In the meantime, I have outright fallen in love with the plantain lilies, and I

Asparagaceae

Hosta plantaginea

have planted many more of them. There are now ten in my garden. They look really glorious in the shady part of the garden – they bring a wonderful magnificence to the shadow. Because of the plantain lilies the shadow appears magnificent, bathed in green light.

In springtime, it is delightful to watch the almost ecstatic growth of plantain lilies. They really have a strong drive. They grow exponentially, and come May already have an impressive size. Their almost eruptive growth made a deep impression on me.

At first, I did not know that plantain lilies, like so many other garden plants, come from the Far East. They are supposed to be indigenous to Korea too, but I have never seen them there. I grew up in the metropolis Seoul. As a child, I did not play in nature, but between a river, which had become a stinking sewer, and railroad tracks. In my childhood memories there are more bad smells than scents. There was no beautiful nature around me. Nevertheless, there were many dragonflies. I particularly liked red dragonflies. In Korean they are called 'chilli dragonflies'. On the blades of grass along the way leading to my school, I also discovered numerous grasshoppers and praying mantises. But that was all the nature for me.

In Korean, plantain lilies are called 옥잠화 (玉簪花). The name comes from a fable: In ancient China, there was a splendid flute player. When once during a moon-lit night he played a beautiful tune, a heavenly faerie appeared to him and told him that the princess in the heavens would like to hear it again. Thus, he played it once more. The heavenly faerie thanked him, pulled a hair pin of jade out of her hair and threw it to him while she rose up into the heavens again. But the flute player was not able to catch it. It fell to the ground and broke into pieces. This made the flute player very sad. At the spot where the hair pin touched the ground, a plant began to grow whose blossom resembled the pin's shape.

The blossoms of plantain lilies are very beautiful. In contrast to the strong leaves, they are extremely delicate and graceful; they seem as fragile as the heavenly faerie's adornment. Especially beautiful are their slightly upwards lifting stamen, reminiscent indeed of old Korean hair pins. As a rule, the blossoms of plantain lilies do not have a scent. But in my garden I have a fragrant plantain lily. It is called *So Sweet*. However, I would not call its scent 'sweet'. It is noble. The scent of the fragrant Hosta is similar to that of a lily but less obtrusive, more reserved, quieter.

I made sure that my plantain lilies have the best possible neighbours. Among these wonderful neighbours are: Caucasian forget-me-nots, astilbes, bellflowers, crane's-bills, grasses, ferns, and for the autumn anemones and baneberries. I would also include foxgloves in the list, two of which grow close to the plantain lilies. All through the summer, the bellflowers create a magnificent blue radiance.

I very much love flowers that love the shade. 'Byung-Chul' means 'bright light'. But without shadow, the light is not light. Without light there is no shadow. Shadow and light belong together. Shadows form the light. Shadows are its beautiful outline.

The Latin name for foxgloves is *Digitalis*. The word 'digital' refers to a finger, *digitus*, which is used for counting. Digital culture makes humans whither into little 'finger beings', so to speak. Digital culture is based on the finger that counts. History, however, is recounting, that is, narrating. It does not count. Counting is a post-historical category. Neither tweets nor information coalesce into a narrative. And a timeline does not tell the story of a life, a biography. It is additive, not narrative. Digital humans 'finger', in the sense that they permanently count and calculate. The digital turns numbers and counting into something absolute. Friends on Facebook are also first of all counted. But friendship is a narrative. The digital age totalizes the additive, counting, and what can be counted. Even affection is counted in the form of Likes. The significance of the narrative dimension is greatly reduced. Today, everything is made countable so that it can be translated into the idiom of performance and efficiency. Numbers make all things universally comparable. Only performance and efficiency can be counted. Thus, everything that cannot be counted ceases to exist. *Being*, however, is a narrating and not a counting. Counting lacks *language*, which is history and remembrance.

I like to water plantain lilies. I observe how the drops of water roll down the broad leaves. Watching flowers while watering them is both calming and pleasing. Watering flowers is a lingering at their side.

In German, plantain lilies are also called Herzlilien (heart lilies) because their leaves are heart-shaped. Their blossoms resemble those of lilies. Plantain lilies perish as fast as they appear. The first frost makes them melt away, so to speak.

Then the astilbes – yes, they deserve some praise. At first, I paid little attention to them. But once they began to flower, I was astonished by their beauty. The colourful panicles have a wonderful sparkle. I had not been aware of their power to shine. It is remarkable that astilbes are also from East Asia. They shine magnificently. Thus, in German they are also called Prachtspiere – 'splendid splinters'. They feel at home in the shade and give it a wonderful splendour, brightness, and festive character.

The literal meaning of 'Spier' is 'small, tender tip'. In principle, the blossoms of all meadowsweets, *Spiraea*, look like this. They are tiny blossoms. Without my garden, I would never have come across the word 'Spier'. Such words widen my *world*. There are not only Prachtspiere but also Sommerspiere (summer splinters) and Harlekinspiere (harlequin splinters).

Then spring came. In May, the plants which during the winter had had barren twigs that looked as if they were dead, or had disappeared altogether save for an unsightly stump, were flowering as if in ecstasy. The garden is an ecstatic place for lingering.

On Happiness

They [plants and animals] are what we were; they are what we ought to become once more. We were nature just as they, and our culture, by means of reason and freedom, should lead us back to nature. They are, therefore, the representation of our lost childhood which eternally remains most dear to us, and thus fill us with a certain melancholy. But they are also representations of our highest fulfilment in the ideal, thus evoking in us a sublime emotion.

Friedrich Schiller, *On Naïve and Sentimental Poetry*[1]

Every day that I spend in my garden is a day of happiness. The present book could also have been called *Essay on Happy Days*. I often long for working in the garden. Previously, I did not know this feeling of happiness. It is also something very physical. I had never been as physically active before. Never had I touched the earth so intensely. To me, the earth seems to be a source of happiness. Many times, I was astonished by its strangeness, its otherness, its independent life. Only in the course of physical work, did I get to know it intensely.

Watching flowers while watering them is calmly delightful, is pacifying. Thus, 'gardening *work*' is not a fitting expression. Work originally means toil and hardship. Gardening, by contrast, brings happiness. In the garden, I recover from the hardship of life.

Ranunculaceae

Anemone hupehensis

Beautiful Names

There are flowers with wonderful, playful, and also mysterious names: Himmelsschlüssel ([heaven's key], cowslip), Tausendschön ([thousand beauties], common daisy), Jungfer im Grünen ([virgin in the countryside], love-in-a-mist), Dame in Trauer ([lady in mourning], mourning iris), Hundszahn ([dog's tooth], dog's-tooth-violet), Brennende Liebe ([burning love], Jerusalem cross), Rührmichnichtan ([touch-me-not], touch-me-not balsam), nightshade. It is almost impossible to learn all flower names by heart. There are said to be 250,000 species in the world. The total number of names would exceed the volume of my German vocabulary several times over.

I used to think a lot about proper names. In my book *Todesarten* (Ways of dying), I wrote:

In a story, Walter Benjamin writes: 'There are, so it is said, seventeen kinds of figs on the island. One ought – the man told himself as he walked in the sun – to know their names.'[1] Thus, every kind of fig is unique and not exchangeable. Their singularity does not permit to call all seventeen kinds of fig by just one name. A general designation would remove their uniqueness, quiddity, their proper name character. Because of this singularity, each kind of fig deserves its own name, a proper name. It deserves to be called, to be called upon by its own name. As if the name would be the fleeting cipher that granted access to the essence, to being, as if only the calling and invocation by their proper name would capture their essence. One would violate the very being of each kind of fig by subsuming their diversity under one single name, one general designation. Only what is singular can be called upon. Only the naming, the invocation by their proper name provides the key to experiencing each kind of fig. What is at stake, mind you, is not knowledge, it is experience. Experiencing is a kind of invocation or evocation. The object of a genuine experience, that is, of the invocation, is not the general but the singular. Only singularity makes encounters possible.[2]

Since I have taken up gardening, I try to remember as many flower names as possible. They have enriched my world considerably. It is probably a betrayal of flowers to have them in one's garden without knowing their names. Without their name it is not possible to invoke them. The garden is also a place of invocation. In this respect Hölderlin's Diotima should be our model:

Amongst the flowers her heart was at home, as if it were one of them. She called them all by name, made them new and more beautiful names out of love and unerringly knew the happiest season of each.[3]

For Nietzsche, naming is an exercise of power. The rulers 'set their seal on everything and every occurrence with a sound and thereby take possession of it, as it were'. Thus, Nietzsche conceives 'of the origin of language itself as a manifestation of the power of the rulers'.[4] Languages are 'after-notes of the oldest appropriations of things'.[5] For Nietzsche, every name is a command: '"thus shall the thing be named from now on!"'[6] Names, accordingly, would be fetters. Naming is appropriation.

I beg to differ. In the beautiful name of a flower I do not hear a command, no claim to power, but love and affection. Diotima, as the giver of names, is a lover. Out of her love for them, she gives the flowers more beautiful names. The names of flowers are *words of love*.

Victoria Amazonica

If Berlin summers were very hot and sultry throughout, and if I had a garden pond, I would love to see
a particular water lily from the Amazonas – *Victoria
amazonica* – flowering on it. By a coincidence, my very
first philosophical talk, which I gave twenty years ago
at the German Philosophical Congress in Leipzig, carried the title *Victoria amazonica*. The paper did in fact
talk about this very beautiful large water lily of the
Amazonas. Back then, I often stayed in Basle. The city
has a small but very beautiful botanical garden, which
also has a water lily house, a greenhouse for tropical
water plants. Once every year, the botanical garden stays
open during the night so that one can admire the *Victoria
amazonica*, which opens its flower at night. This water
lily inspired my philosophical talk. It began with the following words:

There is a water lily from the Amazonas called *Victoria amazonica*. When the sun – Helios, the godfather of *logos* – sets, the thorny flower bud of this water lily rises out of the water and opens up. Its scent attracts insects. After a while, it closes again. For the rest of the night, the locked-up insects linger inside the flower and pollinate it. During the first night, the water lily's flower is white. When opening up again in the second night, it becomes coloured red as if intoxicated. This change in colour is astonishing.

And it ended thus:

For Walter Benjamin, the genuine collector is dazed by objects; he is capable of being inspired by them before possessing them: 'No sooner does he [the collector] hold them [the things] in his hand than he appears inspired by them and seems to look through them into their distance, like a magician.'[1] Heidegger's hand also guards the distance: 'I am thinking of the resting touch of a hand, in which there is gathered something that remains infinitely remote from any feeling grasp. . .'.[2]

A gardener is also a collector. Gardeners allow themselves to be inspired by flowers. I am thinking about the hand of the gardener. What does it touch? It is a loving, waiting, patient hand. It touches what is not there yet. It guards the distance. This makes for the hand's happiness.

I very much would like to have a garden pond. I would like to see a white water lily, a *Nymphaea alba*, flowering in it. But because it is very complicated to create a garden pond, I instead had a nice old limestone trough from

Kaiserstuhl brought to my garden. The stone trough, filled with water, radiates a beautiful tranquillity. Two Japanese goldfish swim in it.

Insects also come to my garden. In Germany, I saw for the first time in my life a large grey dragonfly. They are very nimble. I like it when I come across little grasshoppers while gardening. Around midday, the butterfly bush attracts butterflies. Peacock butterflies love this time of the day. Like many of the other plants, the butterfly bush comes from the Far East. Maybe that is the reason I feel a particular affection for it.

Butterflies and bees are beautiful insects. But there are also insects and other animals which are not beautiful: slugs, earthworms, and woodlice for example. I turn away from them in mild disgust. Because I do not like to kill living beings, I diligently collected the slugs and carried them away. I love all animals and insects. But flies, midges, and slugs pose a challenge for me.

The previous owner of my garden almost exclusively grew dahlias. The first thing I did was to remove them all. There is something common and vulgar about them. They are not noble. And they also attract slugs. Since I removed them, I only rarely spot slugs. I like snails; they carry their own house on their back. They resemble me. They are also as slow and inert as me. Slugs are too naked for my taste, too unhoused. But I do not feel any pity for them because they are too obtrusive for my taste.

In Heidegger's 'earth', strangely enough, there are no insects. In Heidegger, we come across only one kind of insect: the cricket. It is, however, only present as a beautiful sound within the walls of a temple. For Heidegger, insects are probably all vermin [Ungeziefer] in the original sense of the word, that is, animals not suitable to be sacrificed.[3] The animals which Heidegger includes in his earth, his world, are first and foremost sacrificial animals such as roe deer or bulls. I love beautiful insects.

A blackbird with ruffled feathers regularly visits my garden. I recognize it. It is a beautiful visitor. It feels comfortable in my garden. By now I fully identify with it.

Colchicaceae

Colchicum autumnale

Autumn Crocuses

Do not weep when the best withers! soon it will renew itself!
Do not grieve when your heart's melody falls silent! soon
there'll come a hand to make it sound again!
How then was it with me? was I not like a shattered lyre? I
sounded still a little, but they were death tones. I'd sung myself
a sombre swansong! I'd gladly have woven myself a funeral
wreath, but I had only winter flowers.

Friedrich Hölderlin, *Hyperion*[1]

There is great despair in the autumn. Everything withers.
All leaves fall to the ground.

Here and there on trees
a colored leaf or so is seen.
And I stand in front of the trees
often, sunk in thought.

I gaze at one leaf,
hang my hopes upon it;
if the wind toys with my leaf
I tremble to my trembling's limit.[2]

There are extremely beautiful autumn flowers which steadfastly keep flowering into the winter, bindweed for example. I would also count roses as autumn flowers. They cheerily keep flowering until the first frost arrives. They flower into the winter. It is not rare to see tender rose buds with little heaps of snow on them. In my garden I have a few rose varieties which defy the cold with their beauty.

Late autumn does not mean that one has to renounce the glory of blossoms. There are several autumn crocuses, among them *Colchicum autumnale*. In their habitus, autumn crocuses differ very little from spring crocuses. *Colchicum autumnale*, however, has significantly larger blossoms. Its bulbs are also much larger. 'Herbstzeitlose', the one that knows no autumn – what a name! Its enchanting blossom brings a hovering timelessness into the garden. Because of its lushness it does not really fit into late autumn. Everything is destined to decline. And suddenly a large blossom springs up from underneath the fallen leaves. This blossom creates a strange atmosphere in the garden. Where life is dwindling, a new magnificent life awakes. The lessening light and cooler air already announce the nearing winter. But this flower does not obey time. It is probably a metaphysical flower. Its timelessness points to a transcendence. *Colchicum autumnale*, the one that knows no autumn, gives the garden a special kind of melancholy. Again and again, I try to evoke in me this strange garden atmosphere. It is the fundamental mood which holds sway over my garden and which is also the foundation for this book. It at-*tunes* it. Even in spring and summer it does not ebb away. This mood is closely connected with the piano piece from Schumann's *Gesänge der Frühe* to which I listened every day during that time. The longing expectation of the morning, of reawakening life, is the temporal mode of my winter garden.

The first hot summer day of 2016 was the 22nd of April. I was afraid of the approaching end of summer.

Summer was now coming to an end; already I could sense the dreich dank days and the whistling of the winds and the brawling of the rain-swollen streams; and nature, which like a foaming fountain had swelled up in every flower and tree, stood already now before my darkened mind, dwindling and closed down and turned in upon itself, like me.

Hyperion[3]

Asteraceae

Xerochrysum bracteatum

Diary of a Gardener

It's a song for the children
who are born and who live between steel
and bitumen, between concrete and asphalt,
And who will perhaps never know
That the earth was a garden.

There was a garden called the earth.
It shone in the sun like forbidden fruit.
No, it wasn't heaven or hell
Nor anything already seen or heard.

There was a garden, a house made of trees,
With a bed of moss to make love in
And a little rolling stream without a wave
Came to refresh it and continued its course.

There was a garden as big as a valley.
We could eat there in all seasons,
On the burning earth or on the frozen grass
And discover flowers that had no name.

There was a garden called the earth.
It was big enough for thousands of children.
It was once inhabited by our grandfathers
Who themselves got it from their grandparents.

Where is this garden where we could have been born,
Where we could have lived carefree and naked?
Where is this house with all doors open,
That I'm still looking for but can't find anymore?

Il y'avait un jardin (There once was a garden)
Georges Moustaki[1]

E piove su i nostri vólti silvani (And it rains on our forest-like faces)

La pioggia nel pineto (The rain in the pine forest)
Gabriele D'Annunzio

31 July 2016

The sunflowers which I sowed this spring – outside, on the other side of the garden fence – are now flowering despite the glutinous slugs which like their seeds so much. The sunflowers have grown a lot. These sun worshippers surround my garden with their radiant yellow flowers. They seem to be radiant suns themselves. I often look up to them in admiration. They are *tall*. It is a miracle that such a giant plant can grow out of such a tiny seed. I touched the flowering heads and was amazed how solid they felt, how firmly they rested in the ground, how earthy they were. This did me a lot of good and provided me with a beautiful *ground*, which today I need more than ever.

The bindweed at the garden fence blooms purple. The balcony of my flat in Basle, situated near the house where Nietzsche lived, was covered in bindweed. Their flowers opened up early in the morning and closed again in the evening. My balcony was girded by bindweed on the right and vines on the left. In between, cosmoses bloomed in the autumn. At the balcony's right end stood a honeysuckle in a large flower pot. It died with the love that had left. Back then, the clocks also stopped. The pain was great.

The strawflowers bloom gloriously in red, yellow, and white. Their petals feel as dry as straw. They look as if they would never wither. I love their cheerful and carefree nature. They are very child-like. They do not like water at all. When it rains, or I water them, they roll up. You could even say they writhe as if in agony. Sadly, they are annual plants. They bloom only once, never to be seen again. In particular the white strawflower I love.

The blue hibiscus is flowering. Hibiscus is the national flower of Korea. In Korean it is called *Mugungwha*. The blue rose called *Novalis* is also flowering. Blue is the colour of Romanticism. Magnificent [herrlich]. 'Magnificence' ['Herr'], however, does not express its beauty. 'Magnificence' lacks its grace. The blue hydrangea shines modestly in the shade. The berries of *Muscat*

Bleu slowly ripen and turn blue. The Black-eyed Susan is in full bloom. It is the summer flower par excellence. Its smiling eye *shines* throughout the summer into the autumn. It seems so carefree and cheerful.

7 *August 2016*

Monk's pepper is beginning to flower. At first, I thought it might not be winter-hardy because the twigs looked desiccated until the early summer. But to my surprise they sprouted. It was a miraculous resurrection. From dead-looking branches green shoots came forth. They were *alive*! Now they are flowering bright blue.

Monk's pepper is also called chaste tree, lady's bedstraw, or Keuschlamm [chaste lamb] because allegedly it reduces the sexual drive. Thus it symbolizes chastity and virginity. The Goddess Hera, who was born under a monk's pepper tree, got together with Zeus once every year. A bath in the river *Imbrasos* then renewed her virginity. In mediaeval monastery gardens, monk's pepper thrived next to spice and medicinal plants. The monks mixed the hot-tasting seeds into their food as a spice. It did its work as an anaphrodisiac. Other anaphrodisiacs used against 'reprehensible carnal desires' were rue, hops, liquorice, and foxtail (*Amaranthus*). In the first century, the Greek physician Pedanius Dioscorides wrote about monk's pepper:

Agnos, Keuschlammstrauch, known by the Romans as wild pepper, is a tree-like shrub growing along rivers and rocky coastlines. It is called Agnos because at the Thesmophoria the women who kept their chastity

74

Lamiaceae

Vitex agnus-castus

rested on it, and because in the form of a drink it reduces the coital urge.[2]

The apples are getting bigger and more yellow. They taste well. And they have a truly nice smell. The garden is a place of scents. It smells of earth. Strawberries [Erdbeeren], the fragrant berries of the earth [Beeren der Erde], are spreading. Originally, 'Beere' [berry] means 'the red one'. But not all berries are red. I also have white strawberries. The birds do not eat them because they think they are not ripe yet. But they are ripe and taste and smell sweet. Their colour protects them against the greedy birds which gobble up all berries, and also the grapes. This year, the birds are particularly greedy. But they are connoisseurs. They only eat ripe fruit. Cucumber and tomatoes are also there in abundance. They proliferate excessively. I do not like this excessiveness. The Hosta-Plantaginea hybrid *So Sweet* exudes a wonderful fragrance.

12 August 2016

It is a very cold, autumnal day in mid-summer. The flowers, which bloom magnificently despite the cold, compensate for the early departure of summer. This year, it really says good-bye very early. In mid-summer it is autumnal. The autumn flowers begin to appear. The large blossoms of *Colchicum autumnale*, the one that knows no autumn, look like an exotic fruit. They flower festively, even timelessly, in the middle of the autumn. Festive time is timeless. A festival creates timelessness. There are no more *festivals*. Time, therefore, is more transient than ever before. The autumn crocuses bring light and radiance into the otherwise dark autumnal garden.

23 August 2016

I was very sad that because of the short and cold summer the summer flowers so quickly disappeared. They had no time to develop properly. They soon faded away. In the middle of summer, an unexpected coldness introduced a cold and damp autumn. This year, *Colchicum autumnale*, which normally blooms in September or October, bloomed in the middle of summer. One of them looks like a giant crocus; another one has a double flower.

So Sweet, the fragrant hybrid, gives off an intense yet very subtle scent. It smells like a lily. The toad lilies are flowering in the shadow. I love flowers that grow in the shade. I have made the shadow bloom with foxglove, bluebells, plantain lilies, Caucasian forget-me-nots, and Japanese anemones. But it is the hydrangeas which really light up the shadow. They are intoxicating. I love them. I learned to love them over time.

19 September 2016

We are already deep into autumn. The air is very cool. The sorrow is great. Japanese anemones, cosmos, *Colchicum autumnale*, and autumn crocuses are in magnificent bloom. The cosmos seeds I brought back from Korea. So this year Korean cosmos are blooming. Basil, with its alien scent, is apparently also Korean; I bought it at the Perennial Market of the Berlin Botanical Garden.

Monk's pepper, roses, plantain lilies are all slowly losing their vitality and strength to flower. Bluebeard, *Colchicum autumnale*, phlox, blue lobelia, Black-eyed Susan, *So Sweet*, and hydrangeas have lost their colour. The roses and geraniums add a last warm radiance to the garden.

Recently, I have felt as if bleeding to death. The pain made me permeable and vulnerable. My perception sharpened. Somehow everything caused me pain. Then a disaster happened.

There is a beautiful willow in the garden. I love it very much. When I saw one day that it had fallen over I was shocked. Its leaves looked dried out. Apparently, a rodent had gnawed away at its trunk and made a big hole in it. Something red was visible inside it, giving me the feeling that it had bled to death, had left me. It was death announcing itself in my garden.

My willow, my beloved, had bled to death. The wound was so large that it could not be saved. It probably had a premonition that it would die this autumn. In the spring, it had been delirious, circled by a swarm of bees.

On 25 September 2016, I stayed a long time, into the night, with the re-erected corpse of my love, mourned and cried over it, together with the Japanese anemones. The willow bled to death the very moment I thought I would bleed to death. It was my beloved whom I thought I had lost.

29 September 2016

The Japanese autumn anemones, Korean cosmos, and autumn crocuses are flowering magnificently. This year,

Lamiaceae

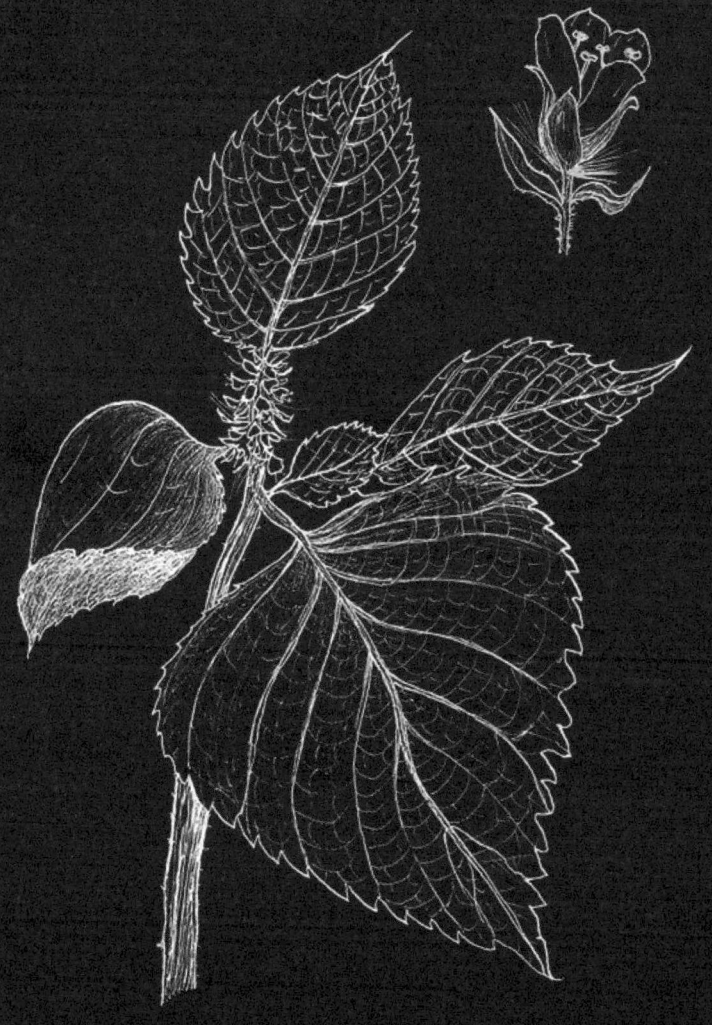

Perilla frutescens

I brought back many seeds for my garden from Korea, first of all the seeds of wild sesame, *Deulkkae*, *Kkaennip* (Japanese: *Egoma*). Its leaves are delicious. I wrap a bit of rice and miso paste in them and eat the lot. It smells lovely. It smells of the earth and its depth and hiddenness. The warmth of the rice harmonizes very well with the spiciness of the sesame leaves. There are many *Deulkkae* recipes. Leaves pickled with soya sauce taste especially nice. They are one of my favourite foods.

Tempura with *Kkaennip* is also delicious. An enticing scent is enclosed in the thin, crispy wrap of dough and released in the mouth. In my book *Absence*, it says:

Tempura, too, follows the principle of emptiness. It does not have the heaviness that typifies fried foods in Western cuisine. In tempura, the oil's only purpose is to turn the very thin layer of batter on the vegetables or fish into a crisp agglomeration of emptiness. The content within also acquires a delicious lightness. If, as in Korea, a tender green sesame leaf is used for tempura, it dissolves in the hot oil and turns into an almost bodiless, fragrant green. It is actually a pity that no cook has yet tried to use a tender green tea leaf for tempura. That would be a delicacy made up of the enchanting smell of tea and emptiness – a delicious dish of absence.[3]

I harvested *Kkaennip* until late autumn. Unfortunately, the plants did not tolerate the frost. They have shrunk and are sagging. The tasty and nicely smelling green has become a black and brown corpse. The plants exude a morbid smell. Monk's pepper, roses, and Hosta slowly lose their vitality and strength to flower.

Bluebeard is flowering beautifully in the shadow. And phlox and garden lobelia are flowering again. The Black-eyed Susan slowly withers and fades. The red geraniums seem to feel comfortable in these cold autumn days.

17 October 2016

There are already plenty of autumn leaves covering the ground. The hydrangeas slowly pale. Their coloured sepals now turn into green leaves. The bluebells, which are neighbouring the hydrangeas, by contrast, are blooming bright purple. Almost stubbornly, the sweet-smelling plantain lily continues to flower. The other lilies have long since produced their seed capsules. I love *So Sweet*, my lily.

In late summer, I had thought that the roses are not doing well this year. They seemed less inclined to flower than in the previous summer, which lay on a bed of roses, so to speak. Now, in the autumn, they are flowering again. The cold even seems to invigorate them. It is particularly nice to watch the roses in the night. *Colchicum autumnale*, which were planted late, are already flowering. Their large double flowers are enchanting.

Gardening teaches me new words that I would never have encountered without it. They often make me happy. There are different species of hydrangeas. Not all are shrubs, some are lianas. I find the word 'liana' extraordinarily beautiful. Liana is the name for a climbing plant with a lignified stem. In my garden, I have two climbing hydrangeas. Hydrangeas have opposite leaves. I find the term 'opposite' [gegenständig] interesting. It refers to phyllotaxis (*phyllon*: leaf; *taxis*: arrangement): the particular arrangement of the leaves. In the case of the opposite type of arrangement, the leaves are in pairs on opposite sides of the stem axis. In the case of the whorled leaves pattern, in German 'quirlständig' or 'wirtelständig', more than two leaves grow at the same height of the stem. The term 'quirlig' I knew, but 'wirtel' was new to me.

Lamina is the name for the plane surface of a leaf above the stalk. The lamina, in turn, is divided into the venation, the vascular bundles, and the intercostal surface areas. The venation of hydrangeas is usually feather-veined, but in some species it is acrodrome. In the case of acrodrome venation the vascular bundles first run parallel to the leaf's edge and then converge towards the leaf's tip. Such foreign words fascinate me. I am often greedy for more of them. It gets ever more complicated and beautiful. The vascular bundles run along the border between the palisade and the spongy parenchyma. When gardening, I am being taken from the German I know so well into a beautiful foreign language, into a beautiful foreign world. Just one leaf harbours so many foreign words. The green leaves of hydrangeas are often *serrated* at the edges. But there are also green leaves with smooth edges. Stipules are absent. Stipules are leaf-like excrescences at the leaf node. Thus, they are mock leaves like *parhelia*, which are mock suns.

I saw three suns stand in the sky.
I watched them long and fixedly.
And they stood there as blank and bright
as if they would not leave my sight.

82

Alas, you cannot be my suns!
Turn then, and gaze at other ones!
Not long ago I'd three of my own;
but now the best two have gone down.

Would that the third might disappear!
In darkness I would better fare.[4]

Hydrangeas have cymous or thyrse inflorescences. One speaks of cyme, or cymous inflorescences, when the main axis ends with a flower. A thyrse inflorescence is created by several cymes on a raceme main axis. Raceme (Latin: *racemosus*) means full of clusters.

A perigynous blossom with superior ovary consists of receptacle, sepals, petals, stamina, and carpels. In hydrangeas, there may also be spathaceous bracts. Around the edge of the inflorescence, there are sterile mock blossoms. Inside, there are fertile, very small, and inconspicuous blossoms. The sterile blossoms have four or five white, reddish, or purple large sepals the size of petals. In many cultivated hydrangeas the fertile blossoms are missing altogether. The mock blossoms, which are usually mistaken for the hydrangeas' blossoms, are not genuine blossoms. They consist of petals. Most fertile blossoms are androgynous. But there are some species that are unisexual. These are dioecious, that is, the male and female flowers are on separate plants.

27 October 2016

It is very wet and cold. The roses bow their heads. They flower with their last remaining strength. The leaves of

Hydrangeaceae

Hydrangea paniculata

the plantain lilies are truly wasting away. Their yellow edges become almost see-through. The green part becomes fully yellow. Amid the autumn leaves, autumn crocuses and *Colchicum autumnale* are flowering. Death and birth, coming and going are mixed up in a deep melancholy. I planted *Colchicum autumnale*, the one that knows no autumn, in September. Their white-purple shoots sprouting out of the ground in late autumn are beautiful. Some 'ground cover plants' (what an unkind expression) keep blooming into the winter. I especially like the creeping forget-me-not, also called blue lobelia. Its flower is bright blue and orchid-shaped. Forget-me-not blooms very reliably.[5] Some of the lavender still has flowers. The yellow coneflower is blooming again. It is interesting that some flowers, having withered, blossom a second time. I like these *latecomers*.

18 November 2016

I am writing these lines at the art nouveau writing desk I recently bought. Its fittings and keys are extraordinarily beautiful. Art nouveau and also art deco are my styles. They have a still, simple, restraint yet buoyant beauty. My new writing desk has a green inlay, a *writing meadow*. Written words blossom on it like wild flowers.

We are deep into the autumn, it is almost winter now. Rain is pouring down. Cold rain. It is very dark, dull, and wet. Even when the sun is out, there is never proper daylight. The sun has lost its power to shine. It looks like a faint disk in the sky. For hours, I raked the autumn leaves. Almost all leaves have fallen by now. I do not like oak leaves at all. They are very crude and robust. Thus, they rot only slowly. I love the softer, weaker leaves which prefer to disappear, to become one with the earth quickly, to return to the earth. Oak leaves are insistent. That is why I do not find them beautiful. I want to burn them quickly.

The hydrangeas look very miserable right now. Their leaves have become brown and black. Everywhere there is putrefaction and decay. Usually, at this time there would be no blooming flowers left in a garden. But my garden is a winter garden. In my garden, a new, second spring is beginning. Everywhere green shoots are sprouting. Autumn crocuses are flowering. The guilder rose is full of buds about to burst. Soon, winter cherry, winter jasmine, winter aconites, pheasant's eye, snowdrops, Chimonanthus, witch hazel, and Christmas rose will be flowering. In my garden, a second spring arrives in the middle of winter.

27 November 2016

Saffron crocus (*Crocus sativus*) is flowering beautifully. It is a crocus that flowers in the autumn. At the centre of the petals are the bright red stigmata, the saffron threads. The yield is very low, however. For a kilogram of saffron one needs more than two-hundred thousand blossoms. Saffron is therefore considered a luxury, the king of spices. It is also believed to be a remedy, and it is used for dyeing precious garments. The Romans were very wasteful with saffron. For them, it represented luxury and lavishness per se. To mark his triumph, Nero had the streets of Rome strewn with saffron.

The saffron crocus seems to love the cold. It flowers in the wintry cold. The narrow, pin-shaped leaves are particularly beautiful. Right now it is flowering not far from a late-blooming white *Colchicum autumnale*. The 'ones that know no autumn' afford the garden a certain time-lessness. They are *Gesänge der Frühe*.

3 December 2016

It is freezing cold. The winter heather is blooming white, yellow, and pink. It does not seem to mind the frost. How patient they are, how well they can bear suffering! They often flower near graves. They promise resurrection. I have picked a crocus blossom and put it in Baudrillard's book *Seduction*.

> There is something impersonal in every process of seduc-tion, as in every crime, something ritualistic, something supra-subjective and supra-sensual, the lived experi-ence, whether of the seducer or his victim, being only its unconscious reflection. Dramaturgy without a subject. The ritual execution of a form that consumes its subjects. This is why the piece takes on both the aesthetic form of a work of art and the ritual form of a crime.[6]

The seductive power of the beautiful girl, its *natural* beauty, must be sacrificed and destroyed by the artful dramaturgy and strategy of the seducer. The art of the seducer, who has no need for psychology, soul, or sub-jectivity, conquers the beautiful girl's natural power to seduce. The seducer is a sacrificial priest who devotes himself to the ritualistic process of seduction.

Today, for a short while, I was able to harbour the illu-sion that it is mid-spring after all. Even in this cold, the pin-shaped leaves of the saffron crocuses shone bright green. The dampness on the grass and the autumn leaves was freezing over and glittered like diamonds, like stars in the clear night sky. I apprehended the silvery shine of the autumn leaves like the shivery skin of a beloved who wants to be warmed by my fingers. I even would have kissed the glittering ground.

A wrinkled apple was still hanging on the leafless apple tree. I noticed it only today and was astonished. It shone yellow in the night. This lonesome winter apple is a present; yes, it praises the earth. It illuminated, released the bleak winter night, as if it were the reflection of a metaphysical light, of a beauty which at the same time represents the good.

12 December 2016

Oak leaves are still lying around everywhere. I hate them. They destroy the forms and colours that make up the garden. They transform everything into the same by eliminating difference. They are dead, but they don't die. They are the undead of my garden. Our society is probably also overgrown with undead who turn everything into the same. German neo-liberalism, for example, can be seen as a kind of ugly forest of oak trees whose undead oak leaves destroy all difference, all otherness between differences. I just notice that the word 'same' [Gleiche] contains the word 'oak' [Eiche].

Almost angrily I removed all the oak leaves from the garden today. Those which were stuck between the twigs of other plants, which had pushed their way into them, I removed one by one, putting them to death, so to speak.

Maple leaves appear nobler and finer to me than oak leaves. I also like the small yellow cherry leaves.

The withered plantain lilies are fully black now. Their leaves are sagging. But they radiate a morbid beauty. Even without flowers, the wintry garden is a magnificent sight to behold. The skeletons of the withered Japanese autumn anemones are just as beautiful as their blossoms. The grasses look particularly attractive in winter. The Christmas roses and camellia shine green next to them. Only winter bloomers retain their deep and rich green. *Sarocca humilis*, also called sweetbox, and Japanese lavender heather, for example, stay green during the winter. I should wrap the camellia in a warm winter coat again. Last year they almost froze to death and only blossomed in spring.

24 December 2016

On Christmas Eve, I was alone in the garden at night. I illuminated the garden with the spotlight I used for shooting my film: I fixed a daylight filter to a halogen lamp; it glows a beautiful white. Daylight is more beautiful than artificial light. During the shooting of my film, *Der Mann, der einbricht* [The man who breaks in], I got to know light. I can now distinguish between beautiful and ugly light. When my dentist looked at my teeth with a magnifying lamp, I interrupted the treatment because the light appeared so beautiful to me. He told me that a colleague had built this magnifying glass especially for him.

The nocturnal daylight transformed the garden into a scene from a film. But it was very bleak in the garden today. Around this time last year, it was very warm.

89

Winter aconites, winter jasmine, and winter cherries were in bloom. All I can see this year are buckled saffron crocuses. Yet, fresh shoots can be seen everywhere. The fragrant guilder rose and winter cherry are close to blooming. The witch hazel will also soon bloom again, red and yellow.

9 January 2017

A bitterly, almost painfully, cold winter day. Temperatures suddenly dropped to below minus ten degrees. The whole of the garden is covered in snow. There is a deep, all-pervasive melancholy. I would love to embark on an eternal winter journey.

Last year, winter aconites, winter jasmine, winter cherry, witch hazel, and fragrant guilder roses flowered between Christmas and New Year. The weather was unusually mild. Thus, there was a spring in the middle of winter.

Today, during the ice cold, frosty night, I suffered a lot with my plants, which I love. I suffered with my beloved ones. Soon, I shall have to protect them against the deadly cold. Camellias need particular care. I shall cover them with my bed cover. There are plants in my garden that have a great need for protection. I want to give them warmth. Love is also solicitude. A gardener is a lover.

19 January 2017

An ice-cold, snow-white night. It is a miracle that some winter bloomers are flowering despite this hostile cold. Witch hazel and Christmas roses are flowering in the snow. They celebrate resurrection. Today is my Easter

Ranunculaceae

Helleborus niger

Day. The flower of the witch hazel shines in cardinal red. The Christmas roses brighten up the night with their white blossoms. It is difficult to tell the white of the snow from the white of the Christmas roses.

29 January 2017

The blossoms of the Christmas roses are shock-frozen, so to speak. Yet, they stubbornly, heroically, keep their shape and colour. Seen in nocturnal darkness, the numerous white buds are beautiful. They bring *Being* into the wintery nothingness. In that sense, they are *metaphysical*. They transcend the physical, which is at the mercy of transience. Their radiance banishes the melancholy of winter. Winter bloomers are sublime, even numinous. They are *numen of my garden*.

On Rilke's gravestone is written: 'Rose, oh pure contradiction, desire'. The Christmas roses in my garden truly are a pure contradiction to death, a flowering resistance to decay and decomposition. They are desire, desire for life, amid the winter's hostility to life. They are almost *immortel*. They embody pure *desire for being*. Their blooming is a delirium, an intoxicating but at the same time melancholic daydreaming in the winter's darkness. Like *Colchicum autumnale*, they create a wonderful time-lessness in my garden.

The ice crystals on the still green frozen grass glitter magically between camellias and witch hazel. The crystals look like stars in the night sky. With delight, I watch the nocturnal display of lights.

In the middle of winter, I long for flowers, for flourishing life. Just now, I miss the flowers a lot. I miss them in an almost physical sense. I even desire them like a lover. In the middle of winter, I long for colours, shapes, and scents.

By now I have reached the conclusion that we have not necessarily become happier as human beings. We become more and more detached from the earth, which could be a source of happiness.

27 February 2017

After a seemingly infinite spell of life-denying coldness, today is the first bright spring day – in the middle of winter. I felt a curious vibration in the air and light. The sun's rays also felt differently. When they fell on my cheek, I sensed the coming, promising spring. The light had a different intensity, a different mood. *Something has changed.* Now the winter aconites are blooming. You can almost watch them grow and open their blossoms. Christmas roses also bloom in abundance. The yellow witch hazel with its subtle fragrance is magical.

The winter bloomers are already attracting bees. Do bees hibernate? All of a sudden, they appear in the middle of winter. They swarm around the Christmas roses and winter aconites. Today I was overwhelmed by this sight. I kneeled down and kissed every blossom. I also kissed the silvery flower bud of the pheasant's eye.

2 March 2017

Today I went again to the – still wintery – garden. I miss the garden particularly at the moment, because especially during the winter it wants to be looked after, wants to be looked at, that is, wants to be loved by me. It is a winter garden in the literal sense. The pheasant's eye carries a silky, silvery flower bud. I was simply overwhelmed by its beauty. Last year, the pheasant's eye did not flower. In some way, my garden has made me a deist. God's existence is no longer a matter of belief for me, but a certainty, just evident. *God is, therefore I am.* I used the knee pad mattress made of foam as my prayer rug. I prayed to God: 'I praise your creation, its beauty. Thank you! Grazie!' Thinking is thanking. Philosophy is nothing but love of beauty and the good. The garden is the most beautiful good, the highest beauty, *to kalon.*

17 March 2017

At the moment, I am in Seoul. I wanted to be close to my dying father.

His sleeping form –
I shoo away the flies today.
There's nothing more to do.

As the day drew to a close, I vainly tried to wet his lips with water from a vessel at his bedside. The twentieth-night moon shone in through the window, and all the neighbourhood was sleeping quietly. As a cock's crow could be heard in the distance announcing the dawn, Father's breathing became increasingly shallow, so shallow that it could hardly be heard.

Issa, *Journal of My Father's Last Days*[7]

Today, I once again visited Seoul's holy mountain, *In-Wang-San*. There is a wintry coldness in Seoul. Nothing green, grey concrete everywhere. On the way to the holy mountain, where gods dwell, I came across flowering winter jasmine. In mid-winter it was flowering bright yellow. This winter blooming shrub obviously loves the mountains. It blooms mainly at heights between 800 and 4500 metres. I felt a deep happiness about this encounter, which seemed like a present from the heavens to me. I picked a few twigs and sacrificed them to the gods of the holy mountain who are no longer given any attention by anyone. But they *are*. The humans around here, on the contrary, worship money. The earth, beauty, the good have disappeared, are completely submerged.

19 March 2017

Today I was with my dying father again. On my way back, I was surprised by a winter blooming tree that I had not known before. It was an Asian cornelian cherry, *Sansuyu*, which is endemic to China, Korea, and Japan. The blossoms look like those of the fragrant guelder rose. I picked a twig. Then I again went to a Buddhist temple on the holy mountain, *In-Wang-San*, and sacrificed the flower to Buddha. I sat in front of the Buddha for a long time and thanked him from the bottom of my heart for the flower. The magnolia in the temple garden already had flower buds. The young Buddhist nuns, *Biguni*, I came across were pure in heart. I played with the small bells that hung on the magnolia. I made a music of tranquillity out of it. Two twin dogs which looked very Korean kept on barking merrily.

21 March 2017

At long last, I am in Berlin again. While in the hellish concrete desert of Seoul, I missed my winter blooming garden very much. In my thoughts, I was always lingering in the garden.

It is astounding that the house into which I recently moved has an inner courtyard in which there are, of all plants, several old shrubs of fragrant guelder roses. Last year, they bloomed as early as December. Their fragrance is magnificent. It filled the whole courtyard. This year, they only blossomed in March. They blossom towards me.

2 April 2017

Chequered lilies, peaches, ornamental plums, and white daffodils are all in bloom. The willow catkins attract a swarm of bees. This year, the camellia did not suffer any frost damage. The winter heather happily continues to bloom. The winter cherry blooms magnificently. Caucasian forget-me-nots shine blue in the shadow. *Saxifraga kabschia* blooms in the background, next to the lavender, which stayed green even during the winter. Daphne blooms lonely, next to the bright pink ornamental plum. This year, the red Christmas roses are blooming. Last year they had no blossoms. Apparently, they have rested and gathered their strength.

Saxifragaceae

Saxifraga kabschia

5 April 2017

While out on a walk, I noticed a magnificent smell in front of an Italian restaurant. A shrub with a wonderful scent was planted in a large pot. I did not know what it was. A guest standing next to the shrub told me that it probably was a beer tree. The proprietor, who did not know the plant's name, told me, presumably because he was embarrassed about his ignorance, that in Italian it is called *Nastro Azzurro*. Back at home, I searched for a tree called *Nastro Azzurro*. Instead of trees, the Italian beer *Nastro Azzurro* appeared on the screen.

I tried to identify the fragrant tree for a long time. Its leaves, which look like a child's hand, helped me to identify it. It is a species of hawthorn. For me, it will always be *Nastro Azzurro*.

9 April 2017

The star magnolia, *Magnolia stellate*, shines brilliant white. The Japanese kerria, or Japanese rose, glows yellow. The chequered lilies enchant the shaded part of my garden. The 'early spring alpine rose', *Rhododendron praecox*, blooms pink. The roses open their leaves. They have a beautiful glossy surface. This year, the roses will bloom magnificently. Roses are so willing to bloom. I am looking forward in particular to the blue rose, *Novalis*.

15 April 2017

The cherry and yellow plum trees bloom magnificently. Their blossoms look similar; they illuminate, even redeem, the still cold April night. Last year, the plums tasted very delicious, earthy-fine-sweet. The tulips are flowering outside the garden fence. They blossom reliably, have a strong floridity. They are dependable and untiring producers of flowers. *Colchicum autumnale* has strong and green leaves which, however, wither and fall off in the summer already, so that it can bring forth its magnificent blossoms in the autumn. The apple tree has reddish flower buds which, however, turn white when opening.

23 April 2017

A bitterly cold night. Despite the late frost – miraculously – not a single plant, not a single flower has been killed. I warmed them with my love. Love is warmth, warmth of the heart, which can withstand the deepest frost.

2 May 2017

For the first time, the lilac is flowering, violet. Its smell is subtle and noble. The apple tree is also flowering. Dawn sets in already half an hour before sunrise. In the early morning, the Schlachtensee, the lake near my garden, glimmers a reddish-grey.

9 May 2017

I find myself right in the middle of today's South Korean presidential elections. This caused me to write the following to a journalist:

Unfortunately, the new Korean president is Moon Jae-in. 文在寅. 在 means 'present'. 寅 means, among other things, 'tiger'. He is very good at shouting. My preferred candidate, Ahn Cheol-soo, cannot shout. But he can think. His name, after all, means: magnificent light. Ahn also means peace. As Adorno said: 'If the lines of our fate become entangled and form an inextricable net, then names are again and again the seals that are imprinted on the lineages . . ., by setting before us initials that we do not understand but obey.'[8]

Moon will divide Korea. In Korean, Moon-jae also means 'problem'. A problematic child, in Korean, is Moon-jae-a 問題児. Moon-jae will not be able to solve Korea's urgent problems 問題. He is a problem himself. Moon-jae 問題. They say that he actually did not want to become president. That he was pushed by his party to stand because he had been a member of staff under the previous president, Roh Moo-hyun. The latter I appreciate a lot. Moon has no class. After his victory, he used a gesture to make fun of Ahn Cheol-soo. In the final days before the election, Ahn Cheol-soo wanted to be close to the people. He walked with a backpack and trainers through the realm of the nation. I was very touched by this. I would have walked with him and would have helped him with my words. After his defeat, I let him know through Korean journalists that at the next election I would stand by his side and speak and shout for him. He himself is not good at shouting. He appears to be very quiet and peaceful.

These presidential elections were a highly complex affair. The West simplified it by reducing it to the tension between North Korea and the US. The German

Asia correspondents do not even speak the national languages. Thus, they read the *Yonhap News Agency* which is faithful to the government, or they use interpreters whose German, however, is not good. The reports, accordingly, are poor, even distorting. They report for instance that Moon would continue the 'sunshine politics' of Kim Dae-jung. But especially during the period of this sunshine politics, North Korea intensified work on nuclear bombs and rockets. Probably with money that Kim sent to the North. His Nobel Peace Prize, it is said, has in a certain sense been bought with a lot of money. The real problem is not the Kims of North Korea, the real problem is the US.

During the presidential elections, morning glories are said to have bloomed magnificently in the garden of Ahn Cheol-soo's parents. Ahn spoke of the 'good tidings of the flowers'. In Korean, morning glories are called 나팔꽃. They promise good things. Maybe Ahn Cheol-soo was also the flowers' preferred candidate. I love morning glories, especially the blue ones. They open at dusk and bloom into late autumn.

Floral greetings from my garden which is in magnificent bloom just now, despite the coldness.

Morning glories stand not only for good news but also for lost love and for faithfulness. According to a fable, it is the flower of faithfulness. A famous painter is said to have had a very beautiful wife. Her fame also became known to the prince. He decided to rob the painter of his wife. He accused him of a crime and put him in prison. Over the longing for his wife the painter lost his mind. Later, he

101

locked himself up in his house and painted picture after picture, until one day he died next to his paintings. He appeared to his beloved in a dream. And when she opened the window, expecting her beloved, she saw a morning glory in front of her house.

14 May 2017

Today, I got sore skin from weeding. There is a heart-shaped abrasion on the palm of my right hand. It hurts a lot. But then, I hurt the 'weeds' too. I weeded them sore. After all, as a gardener I have to take care that none of the plants grow too rampantly. A few daisies, I find beautiful. I will not remove them from the garden. But I have an aversion to certain plants which are very destructive and ruthless. They push out the noble but weak plants. There is a particular kind of clover I especially hate. It even appears to me in my dreams, or daydreams, and tortures me. It is indestructible. It overgrows everything. It spreads like skin cancer. It is not enough to remove the leaves above ground. One must pull out the roots – very tedious work.

18 May 2017

The rhododendron is flowering for the first time. I looked after sick roses today. Their leaves are rolling up. This is caused by larvae of the rose sawfly, despite its name actually a kind of wasp. I planted a beautiful tree, the *Cornus* (dogwood). I again stayed in the garden until dawn. The myriads of yellow-shining gorse illuminate the night and make me happy.

26 May 2017

A wonderful summer day. The roses are beginning to bloom. I dived deep into the delightful warmth of the light.

Why do roses have prickles? You would anyhow not touch a beautiful rose, simply out of reverence. I approach them with great devotion and stoop over them full of awe and respect. I would not want to touch them. Their beauty commands distance.

> Exhausted, I sought
> a country inn, and found
> wisteria in bloom
>
> Matsuo Bashô[9]

8 June 2017

The roses are blooming as if enraptured. Some branches bend down deep under the weight of the flower heads. At the entrance to the garden, a field poppy is blooming. This year, I have many poppies in the garden. The black peony poppies, *Papaver paeoniflorum*, with their double flowers are especially attractive. Reliably, the yellow lilies are blooming again. They are keen to bloom. Honeysuckle blooms in purple. Its flower possesses a playful grace.

12 June 2017

The plantain lilies are blooming. They make me feel happy and exhilarated. The fragrant plantain lily, by contrast, does not yet bloom. The different leaves of the lilies are so beautiful. Actually, they are more beautiful than their very unassuming blossoms.

14 June 2017

I have removed the dead willow from the garden. Almost fervently, I again cursed the evil rodent which killed the most beautiful tree, my beloved. It was a brutal murder.

17 June 2017

A fresh summer day. I do not like heat. The astilbes glow. The blossom of St John's wort shines yellow. The flower beds have been cleared of weeds. Thus, they gain more of a shape.

19 June 2017

The Wannsee glistens deep blue in the summer night. The violet larkspur is tall, even towers above the roses. Presently, the nights are very short. And it never gets fully dark. Somewhere at the horizon, a glimmer of light always remains. These bright nights are beautiful. I have harvested the cherries. They taste sunny. The dark red strawberries taste delicious – as opposed to the strawberries you get in the shops.

The nocturnal opulence of blossoms is elating. Today, in the middle of summer, I took a hot bath with fragrant water lilies. For the first time, Sargent's hydrangea, *Hydrangea sargentiana*, in German commonly called the 'velvet hydrangea', has flower buds. For two years, it was

Papaver paeoniflorum

unwell. I cared lovingly for it. Now it reciprocates my love.

21 June 2017

Today was the first time that I have seen olive trees in bloom not in Italy but here in Berlin at an Italian restaurant in my neighbourhood. They bloom in Schöneberg, actually on the Schöneberg. They are planted in pots and stand in front of the restaurant. Outside, they would not survive the cold and rough Berlin winter. The olive blossoms are very small. They resemble the fertile blossoms of hydrangeas and, like them, they form an umbel. My pasta dish with mushrooms was delicious. And so were the light-green olives in the salad.

25 June 2017

Today I dressed the yellow plum tree in a net. I wanted to protect the delicious plums against the birds. Two years ago, they ate every single one of the grapes which I had wanted to watch slowly maturing. The birds were glutinous, or just greedy for the grapes. But this year, the grapes remained strangely untouched. No birds were to be seen. This, in turn, also made me feel very sad and uneasy. Why don't you come here, my birds, here you can get delicious grapes! This year, there are also only very few bees. I very much hope that the butterfly bush will soon bloom and attract beautiful butterflies again. It is metres high this year. The day lilies are thriving. Their yellow and red flowers *shine*. Yes, *shining* is the right verb for flowering day lilies. Roses do not shine. They require a different verb. Anemones and strawflowers shine. And roses? They also do not gleam because there is something hesitant about them. Roses are reserved. This is what makes for their magnificence. Roses rose. 'To rose', that is the right verb for them.

Rilke loved roses and angels. There are many roses in my garden. They gently let go of my eyes. And at the entrance to my garden, there are two statues of angels. They protect my rose garden. Rilke wrote many poems about roses:

Rose, oh pure contradiction,
desire, to be no one's sleep
under so many lids.

Night made of roses, night made of many, many
bright roses, bright night of roses,
sleep of a thousand eyelids of roses.
Bright sleep of roses, I am your sleeper

Bright sleeper of your scents; deep
sleeper of your cool intimacies.

And then, like this: that a feeling arises,
because blossom leaves stir blossom leaves?
And this: that one opens up like an eyelid,
and beneath lies eyelid after eyelid,
closed ones, as if, ten times asleep
they had to dampen down an inner power of vision.[10]

At the moment, I love these lines on roses because I have difficulties sleeping and long for a deep but bright sleep, a *rose sleep*. I would love to sleep myself away into a no one, into something nameless. That would be a form of redemption. Today, we occupy ourselves only with our egos. Everyone wants to be someone, loud; everyone wants to be authentic, be different to others. Thus, everyone is like everyone else. I miss the nameless.

In his famous *Letter on 'Humanism'*, Heidegger writes:

> But if the human being is to find his way once again into the nearness of being he must first learn to exist in the nameless. In the same way he must recognize the seductions of the public realm as well as the impotence of the private. Before he speaks the human being must first let himself be claimed again by being, taking the risk that under this claim he will seldom have much to say.[11]

We have a lot to say, a lot to communicate because we are *someone*. We have forgotten silence and how to keep silent. My garden is a place of silence. *I make silence* in my garden. I *listen*, like Hyperion.

> My whole being stills and listens when the gentle ripple of the breeze plays about my breast. Often, lost in the immensity of blue, I look up into the aether and out into the hallowed sea, and it's as if a kindred spirit opened its arms to me, as if the pain of isolation were dissolved in the life of the godhead. To be one with everything, that is the life of the godhead, that is the heaven of man.[12]

Digitalization intensifies the noise of communication. Not only does it destroy stillness but also the haptic,

108

the material, scents, radiant colours, and most of all the *heaviness of earth*. 'Human' is derived from *humus*, earth. The earth is our resonance space, it brings us happiness. When we leave the earth, happiness leaves us.

There is a close connection between the analogue and the haptic. The analogue world is graspable and visible. In the film on Vermeer, *Girl with a Pearl Earring*, there is a beautiful scene about the mixing of colours. The protagonist is enthusiastic about the beauty of matter. It is wonderful to see how paints are produced and sold, like spices in an exotic food shop. The blue crystal used in producing Vermeer blue, ultramarine, is divine. The colours used by Vermeer cannot be artificially created. They were made from stones. The stones were ground like spices. The ground materials also look just as edible as spices. Powders and pastes are mixed up. The texture of the material is also enigmatic. A pigment made of grapes is called 'wine corrosive' [Weinätze]. Even the excrement of beetles is used to produce a colouring agent. One of the colours looks like olive oil but is made of bull's urine. Colours are fragrant.

Digitalization ultimately does away with reality as such. Or reality is de-realized and becomes a window within the digital. The time will soon come when our field of vision resembles a three-dimensional display. We move away from reality more and more. My garden, for me, is *reality regained*.

30 June 2017

Yesterday, Berlin was hit by torrential rain, a once-in-a-century meteorological event that turned the city into a landscape of lakes. Once the heavy rain had ended, I went to the garden. I was very concerned about all my loved ones. The sky was still grey. The Wannsee glistened greyish. Apparently, the rain had not done any harm to my plants. It had had a soothing effect on them. Today, they all prosper and bloom magnificently. The hydrangeas are breathtakingly beautiful, especially the panicled hydrangea, Vanilla fraise. The garden intoxicates me with its lush beauty. It is a luxury to have it. Only the roses drop their heads. All other plants are richly green and bloom magnificently. The blossoms of the plantain lilies bulge. They look so refreshed, enlivened and happy after the rain. Apparently, they love rain.

1 July 2017

The panicled hydrangea with its fertile blossoms is enchantingly beautiful. The Sargent's hydrangea is flowering for the first time. For two years, it had been unwell. This year, I changed the soil around it and added some fertilizer. Now it seems to have enough strength to bloom.

I love shade-tolerant plants. But I also love roses. As opposed to me, they love the sun. My temperament is probably not sunny. I like to linger in the shade, in the bright shade, in shadowy light. There is something mysterious about the plantain lilies, something unfathomably deep. I identify most with plantain lilies and hydrangeas.

10 July 2017

The bright crescent moon shines
from behind the old pine tree –
The capers quietly keep on blooming

I have left my beloved garden near the Wannsee for two
weeks so that I can be in the Mediterranean landscape
again. 'Mediterranean' literally means 'amid the earth'.
Thus, here I am particularly close to the earth. *Nearness
to the earth* is exhilarating. The digital medium, however,
nullifies the earth, this wonderful creation of God. I love
the terrestrial order. I will not leave it. I feel a sense of
deep allegiance, a deep connection with this valuable gift
of God. Religion, I think, means nothing but this deep
connection which, however, sets me free. Being free does
not mean buzzing around or being uncommitted. At the
moment, freedom for me is *lingering in the garden.*

Here in Italy, there is an age-old tree at the garden
entrance. I was very astonished when I realized that it was
a blackberry. I had only known blackberries as shrubs.
Thus, this blackberry tree, which is probably a few hun-
dred years old, has an *alien beauty.* It makes me very happy.
Simply looking at it is healing, simultaneously relaxing
and redeeming. I think it must have grown in the Garden
of Eden next to myrtle, laurel, and cinnamon trees. Thus,
I am amid the landscape of *Hyperion.*

The whole day and the whole night, until the dawn of
day, I am now sitting next to the blackberry tree. Next to
it (I am staying on a slope near Mount Vesuvius), there
is an age-old olive tree. The cottage, however, is surrounded by a hedge of *Bougainvillea.* Its flowers are very

111

Moraceae

Morus rubra

much like those of hydrangeas. The bright purple leaves that are often mistaken for the flowers of *Bougainvillea* are actually foliage. These colourful and shiny composite flowers are called spathaceous bracts. They surround two or three very small white fertile blossoms. As opposed to hydrangeas, the *Bougainvillea* loves sunshine. It is almost greedy for it. The *Bougainvillea* may be enticingly beautiful, but it is not mysterious. It lacks hidden depth. I love shade-tolerant plants such as hydrangeas or plantain lilies. I think my fragrant plantain lily will now be blooming in my absence.

Looking at the beautiful sight of Vesuvius and the Gulf of Naples, I drink, almost throughout the day, a red wine from the Campania region, called *Lacryma Christi*: the tears of Christ. It is the wine of Vesuvius. Slowly I begin to understand Christ's pain. However, I also love the *Angelico*, also from Campania. It has an angel-like taste. The vineyards are situated here on the slopes of the volcano. In past times, the monks of the local monasteries pressed the wine. It has a depth that one could call *holy*. Next to my cottage, there are a few vineyards.

And if I cried, who'd listen to me in those angelic
orders? Even if one of them suddenly held me
to his heart, I'd vanish in his overwhelming
presence. Because beauty's nothing
but the start of terror we can hardly bear,
and we adore it because of the serene scorn
it could kill us with. Every angel's terrifying.

Rainer Maria Rilke, *Duino Elegies*[13]

113

The godless Neapolitans who use the holy mountain as a landfill site and set fire to it, God would punish harshly; he would suffocate them with black ash as once happened in Pompeii. Divine punishment certainly is cruel but it is healing. Vesuvius will *rule supreme* again.[14] Its violence is of a different kind compared to that of humans. It is *purifying*. I can understand Hyperion's pain among the Greeks who have become godless. In front of the altar, I recited D'Annunzio's poem *Ho pregato a lungo*, this divine song of the earth.

Watching the morning dawn, the awakening light next to the sea makes one feel at once intoxicated and happy. Vesuvius awakes. It is still veiled in smoke. It burns.

The narrow path leading to my cottage by the sea is lined with caper bushes. They jump out of the walls, so to speak. The flowers of capers have a magic beauty. They almost *beam*. Mimosas have a similar flower. It is shy; it beams from out of a hidden place.

Caper berries are one of my favourite foods. I will soon harvest them and take them with me to Berlin. They need to mature several months in vine vinegar.

Every day, with Mount Vesuvius in sight, I play Bach's *Goldberg Variations*. I had a piano put up in my cottage by the sea. The brand is called *Horugel*. But the Italians do not pronounce the consonant 'h'. On the phone, the man renting out pianos in Naples said that the piano was an 'orugel', an organ.[15] I need a piano not an organ, I replied. The piano sounds acceptable. But it lacks depth and inwardness. Every day, I play Bach in my garden by the sea.

The Mediterranean landscape is intimate. It touches me in my innermost being. The flapping of a black bird's

114

Capparaceae

Capparis spinosa

wing permeates me. It touches me deep down. Everything here is very close, very intimate. 'Intimus' is the superlative of 'inter'. I am right in the middle of the landscape.

12 July 2017

For the first time, I gave a lecture in Italy. I began by citing, in Italian, a poem by Gabriele D'Annunzio, *La pioggia nel pineto* (The rain in the pine forest):

Taci. Su le soglie	Quiet. At the edge
del bosco non odo	of the forest you don't hear
parole che dici	words as spoken
umane; ma odo	by humans; you hear
parole più nuove	much fresher words
che parlano gocciole e	that speak of droplets and
foglie	leaves
lontane.	in the distance.
Ascolta. Piove	Listen. Rain
dalle nuvole sparse.	from scattered clouds.
Piove su le tamerici	Rain on the tamarisks
salmastre ed arse,	all salty and parched,
piove su i pini	rain on the pine trees
scagliosi ed irti,	all scales and bristles,
piove su i mirti	rain on the myrtles
divini,	divine,
su le ginestre fulgenti	on the gorse
di fiori accolti,	shining with flowers,
su i ginepri folti	on the junipers covered
di coccole aulenti,	with nests of fragrant berries,
piove su i nostri volti	rain on our
silvani,	sylvan faces,

116

piove su le nostre mani	rain on our
ignude,	naked hands,
su i nostri vestimenti	on our
leggieri,	light clothes
su i freschi pensieri	on the fresh thoughts
che l'anima schiude	opened up by the soul
novella,	for the first time,
su la favola bella	on the beautiful tale
che ieri	you followed
t'illuse, che oggi m'illude,	yesterday, I follow today,
o Ermione.	oh Hermione.
Odi? La pioggia cade	You hear? The rain falling
su la solitaria	on the lonely
verdura	green,
con un crepitío che dura	the persistent rustling
e varia nell'aria	filling the air, and
secondo le fronde	varying in accord with
più rade, men rade.	thinner and thicker branches.
Ascolta. Risponde	Listen. To the wailing
al pianto il canto	responds the
delle cicale	cicadas' song,
che il pianto australe	not frightened
non impaura,	of the southern wailing,
nè il ciel cinerino.	nor of the ashen sky.
E il pino	And the pine
ha un suono, e il mirto	has its timbre, and the myrtle
altro suono, e il ginepro	another timbre, and the juniper
altro ancóra, stromenti	yet another, diverse
diversi	instruments
sotto innumerevoli dita.	below countless fingers.
E immersi	And immersed

117

noi siam nello spirto	we are in the sylvan
silvestre,	spirit,
d'arborea vita viventi;	the vivacious arboreal life;
e il tuo volto ebro	and your face soaked
è molle di pioggia	and soft from the rain,
come una foglia,	like a leaf,
e le tue chiome	and your hair
auliscono come	it smells like
le chiare ginestre,	the clear gorse,
o creatura terrestre	oh creature of the earth
che hai nome	whose name is
Ermione.	Hermione.[16]

The protagonist in my film *Der Mann, der einbricht* [The man who breaks in] was meant to recite this poem. But he did not succeed in reciting it. Today, I *sang* the poem by D'Annunzio in Italian. For the poem is a *Song of the Earth*. It must be *sung*.

17 July 2017

Today, I went to the Santa Chiara Monastery. In the silent cloister with hand-painted majolica there stood an orange tree. I picked up an orange from the ground. Its scent was wonderful. I want to take it back to Berlin and remember the earth of Naples. But exhaust fumes of godless humans pollute the fragrant earth.

In the dome, I was blessed by a Franciscan. His name was Giuseppe. We embraced. My baptismal name is Alberto. Many people in Italy are called Alberto. A taxi driver in Naples was called Alberto. He told me my Saint's day was 7 August. I should not forget it. At the church in

Nyctaginaceae

Bougainvillea

Korea I was called Alberto. The Catholic church was right next to my house. I was born into faith, even *sheltered by it*.[17] Every day I recited the rosary. The nun who adorned the altar with flowers often gave one of them to me and my sister when we were sitting on the steps in front of our house during the day. Thus, we called her the sister of flowers. She was beautiful and *good*.

Inside the dome at the Piazza Santa Chiara, I was filled with the Holy Spirit that shone brightly at the altar. But the people here are shy of light, or they are blind to the light. The tourists take selfies in front of the altar, in front of the Holy Spirit which actually makes one selfless. Spirit is love and reconciliation. I tried to chase these inconsiderate tourists away. Some of them protested heavily against my wrath. I can understand that Jesus chased away the money changers from the Temple Mount. Money destroys the spirit. The earth is precious and priceless. But humans destroy it because of money. What an infamy!

20 July 2017

When the morning dawns, it is nice to wander around in the garden and look at the plants. Again and again, I am amazed by their sublimity.

I never really liked ivy; it grows across graves and walls. I love shade-tolerant plants, but only those that shine brightly. Astilbes, for example, shine pink. Until now I always thought that ivy lacks luminosity. In the garden by the sea, it appears in an altogether different light because of its bright white blossoms. Originally, I thought that ivy has only dark green leaves and does not blossom. Today

I saw flowering ivy and admired its beauty. Its beauty glows. The ivy's not yet opened flower buds have a fluff with a silky shine. I fell in love with these buds. I love the ivy's hidden brilliance.

In antiquity, ivy was a symbol for intoxication. I recall that in Plato's *Symposium*, ivy is associated with intoxication:

Alcibiades appears – drunk, crowned with ivy and violets (the insignia of Dionysus), adorned with ribbons in his hair, and accompanied by night owls and the female flute player who had been sent away at the beginning of the symposium.[18]

Ivy is indestructible. But it is also a symbol for love and faithfulness. Tristan and Isolde were buried separately after their death-in-love. But out of their graves, they say, ivy trailed and re-united the two in love. Ivy has a special vital rhythm that endears it to me. Only after many years does it blossom right into the winter. Its blossoms attract bees and butterflies. Especially the beautiful *admiral* with its splendid black and red colours loves them.

21 July 2017

All of a sudden, the caper berries turned red and popped open, as if drunk. The seeds inside are black. I picked some of the red caper berries and extracted the seeds from the very squidgy slime. Hopefully, they will sprout and grow out of the wall, maybe only for one summer. They will probably not survive the winter in Berlin.

Being far away from my garden, I want to talk about a few plants in it that I have not mentioned yet. I planted a Korean fragrant guelder rose with reddish-pink flower buds: *Viburnum carlesii*. Not far from it stands a Japanese umbrella pine, *Sciadopitys verticillata*. After it was inactive for a long time, this year its circumference grew noticeably. The new shoots are light green. Also very beautiful is the white monkshood, *Aconitum napellus*. Of an unassuming beauty is the shrubby cinquefoil, *Potentilla fruticosa*. Saxifrage thrive in the sunny corner between the stones. They love stones. The literal meaning of saxifrage is 'stonebreaker'. The Chinese beautyberry, *Callicarpa bodinieri*, carries really nice fruits that shine like violet pearls. On the Staudenmarkt at Berlin's botanical garden I bought a Korean basil, *Houttuynia cordata*.[19] It has a peculiar fleshy scent. Its actual name is chameleon plant or Chinese lizard tail.

At the edge of the garden grows the alpine rose (*Rhododendron praecox*), which flowers very early in the year. Dogtooth violet, *Erythronium dens-canis*, flowers in the shade. It is a *Liliaceae*. The sedge, *Carex baldensis*, which I planted next to the limestone trough, is very graceful. At one point, I had two Japanese goldfish in the stone trough. Shortly before the winter set in, I had to release them into the Wannsee. In the garden's shady part, Asian bleeding heart, *Dicentra spectabilis*, is shining. There are many herbs in my garden: woodruff, thyme, coriander, mint, basil, and parsley. The lavender is indestructible. It flowers into late autumn. In the winter, I rub the leaves between my fingers and smell them. The scent is very calming. I also like the scent of green lavender cotton, *Santolina viridis*.

Saururaceae

Houttuynia cordata

23 July 2017

Thankfully, Vesuvius is no longer burning. Its outlines can be seen clearly again. Every day, I swim towards Vesuvius. It is a delight to look at the sea and the tall black mountains at the horizon. I cover my feet with the warm sand and rub the small seashells between my fingers. Lizards rush across the wall. They clearly love the earth and its warmth.

Today I swam towards a seagull with a yellow beak. It sat still on the water. When I tried to touch it, it flew away. Seagulls are very graceful birds.

25 July 2017

I am back in Berlin. In my Neapolitan garden by the sea I felt a divine warmth. The old mulberry tree which I first mistook for a blackberry was a blessing that gave me deep delight. Staying at the sea was beautiful and *pacifying*. Only the pungent stench of the human, of the all-too human, that lay over Naples, disturbed the fragrant stillness in nature.

I will soon pickle the caper berries I harvested. The buds, the actual capers, have a finer taste than the caper berries. But both have the same scent.

On the flight back, I felt as if I was flying over an endless desert of ice. Some bulging clouds looked like icebergs. Thus, the return flight to Berlin was a special kind of winter journey.

Shortly before midnight, I rushed to my garden at the Wannsee, as if to a beloved daughter I had left alone for two weeks. I could not wait until the next morning. I had a sense of commitment and love for my garden.

I have never before experienced such rainfall in Berlin. The rain was pouring down like a waterfall. After two weeks without rain, the rain did me good. For D'Annunzio, I thought, the rare rain must have possessed a special, even divine, value, like *Lacryma Christi*. Thus, rain can be a blessing:

Forests spread
Brooks plunge
Rocks persist
Mist diffuses

Meadows wait
Springs well
Winds dwell
Blessing muses.[20]

Winds dwell? That is not true, actually. *Winds wander.* Heidegger, his *heart*, however, was rather grounded [bodenständig]. He loved standing not wandering. He was a Greek-German thinker. Zhuangzi, by contrast, loved wandering. His *Song of the Earth* would be:

Forests rest
Brooks flow
Rocks tower
Rain falls

Meadows linger
Wells rush
Winds wander
Blessing grounds.

In the pouring rain I looked at my flowers. My torch, which I like to misuse as a spotlight for my camera, made them look even more beautiful.

The sight of the hydrangeas in lush bloom intoxicated me. They love the rain. The buds of Sargent's hydrangea first have a bulb-like form. Then they unfold into glorious splendour. They almost explode, like a firework in slow-motion. Their beauty is indescribable.

I cut roses in the rain. Roses do not like rain. I wish them a lot of sunshine. Plums, apples, and grapes are slowly maturing. The redcurrants already taste delicious. Because of the lasting dampness, some large mushrooms grow underneath the plum tree. They may be poisonous, but they have an earthy scent. This scent is soothing. I would have liked to eat them. The fragrant plantain lily is not yet in bloom. It is probably a late bloomer that makes up for its lateness by flowering until the threshold to winter. The violet blossoms of the bellflowers sound their trumpet, so to speak, brightly into the night. The smell of lavender perfumes the rainy day. At the moment, the butterfly bush also suffers because of the rain. This year, only a few butterflies came to visit.

Today, I was too occupied with the not-so-pleasant world and missed the lunar eclipse. How stupid!

11 August 2017

The apples have grown a lot. Plums are slowly maturing. Their golden radiance is beautiful to behold. They taste sour. The butterfly bush is still in bloom. A brimstone butterfly and a peacock butterfly are sitting motionless on a light purple umbel.

Suddenly there is the hum of a large grey dragonfly next to my ear. It was here the previous year as well. Maybe it is a good omen. As a child, I caught dragonflies with a butterfly net, but always released them again. I did not understand the violence exercised by my accomplices who mutilated them. I also liked to go fishing. The fish I caught, I also released again. Angling was only a form of meditation. Work in the garden is not really work but meditation, a lingering in stillness.

The fragrant plantain lily is flowering. This year, oddly, it does not smell. Has it been too moist? It is actually a fragrant late bloomer. The yarrow looks nice. It resembles hydrangeas. I did not plant it. It visited my garden as a 'weed' and delighted me. There are other 'weeds' which I happily accept in the garden because they are beautiful. And they do not grow excessively. They too are *solitary creatures*.

15 August 2017

There are flowers that look peculiar or whimsical. In the inner courtyard of my apartment in Berlin grows a shrub with whimsical blossoms. They look like red Chinese lanterns. First, I thought it was an *Asian bleeding heart*. But it was not. It looks like an exotic lamp-shade with four bobbins hanging down as an adornment. In my garden, I have a Chinese lantern, *Physalis alkekengi*. Next to the cosmoses it radiates red into the autumn.

Liliaceae

Fricyrtis japonica

21 August 2017

The fragrant plantain lily is flowering. I love this late blooming lily. *Everything* that is *late* has a scent. The toad lilies are beginning to bloom. They are also late bloomers. The autumn anemones shine white and pink. The chaste tree quietly shines into the autumn. The Korean basil has very peculiar blossoms. It has white piston-shaped pistils with four white spathaceous bracts. Herbs often have beautiful blossoms. Next year, I shall sow Korean mint. As opposed to the native species, it is said not to grow profusely. I do not like plants that grow rampantly.

25 August 2017

It is a damp and cold autumn day. It already *autumns*. The plums are dark yellow and taste delicious. There are plenty of them this year. The apple tree, by contrast, seems not to be well. It carries only a few apples. This year, they taste sour and bitter. Apparently, it missed the sun. The Japanese umbrella pine has grown considerably this year and sparkles bright green.

At the moment, the world seems to drown in torrential rain, following devastating forest fires. Humans wreck the earth. Now they receive the punishment for their ruthlessness and unreason. What is needed more than ever today is *praise of the earth*. We need to spare the earth. Otherwise, we will perish because of the destruction we wage.

Yet where danger lies,
Grows also that which saves

Friedrich Hölderlin[21]

29 August 2017

Today is a sunny, yet already very autumnal day. The roses are still willing to bloom. Intrepidly, they carry on blooming. I cut them back once more. The hydrangeas are carrying their last blossoms. They have lost a lot of their colour and shine. Slowly their colourful composite flowers pale. This year, the late-blooming white hydrangea with pink edges is a particularly beautiful sight. It flowers half hidden between the plantain lilies.

Especially in the winter, the dried flower umbels of the hydrangeas look beautiful. They are the most beautiful winter flowers that keep me happy throughout the winter. I appreciate their morbid beauty. Standing next to the rich green shoots in spring, they look especially enticing.

Among the fragrant flowers, the late-blooming fragrant plantain lily has the most beautiful scent. No other flower in my garden has such a delicate, reserved, noble, and fine scent. I would love to smell like it.

3 September 2017

Although the Black-eyed Susan is still blooming here and there, the days are very cool by now. The chaste tree continues to bloom with dignity. It illuminates the autumn. The most beautiful flowers are presently the tall white hibiscus and the Japanese autumn anemone. I would name the latter the perennially shining one: *Coruscis perennis*. Hibiscus has a great amount of grace and purity. Like many other beautiful flowers, it comes from Asia.

My secret garden, thus, is a *Far East Garden*. The winter-sweet, or Japanese allspice, *Chimonanthus praecox*, which has been part of my garden for three years now, still holds back with regard to flowering. It is said to have a beguiling scent. I hope next year it will flower. *Hoping* is the temporal mode of the gardener. Thus, my *Praise of the Earth* is directed at the *coming earth*.

20 November 2017

It is freezing cold today. It rains and hails. Shortly before dawn, I went to the garden again. The autumn leaves cover the ground knee-high. The winter cherry blooms almost ecstatically, as if it were spring. The white panicled hydrangea is still blooming. It is incredible that it still blooms in this winter cold. Other hydrangeas have completely withered. The roses maintain their form and colour, almost stubbornly. With white frost on them, they look especially enchanting.

The involucre of the Chinese lantern plant has by now become fully translucent. Through its delicately woven skeleton you can see the red fruit. Overall, it looks like a precious jewel. The earth is an artist, a gambler, and a seducer. She is romantic. She evokes a feeling of gratitude in me. And she has made me think a lot. Thinking is thanking.

As a child I turned the fruit of the Chinese lantern plant into a small balloon by carefully emptying it. You can play with it in your mouth and also produce sounds with it. I have a piece of childhood in my garden.

The Chinese beautyberry has purple pearls that shine when morning dawns. The earth is beautiful, even

Calycanthaceae

Chimonanthus praecox

magical. We should spare her, treat her well; we should praise her instead of brutally exploiting her. Beauty obliges us to treat her with care. I have learned this and experienced it.

List of Illustrations

NOTES

Preface

1 Laozi, *Daodejing*, no. 29 (MWD 73), Oxford: Oxford University Press, 2008, p. 61.

Winterreise

1 Franz Schubert, *Winterreise* [Winter journey], song no. 11: 'Dream of Springtime'. Quoted after Hampsong Foundation, transl. William Mann, available at https://hampsongfoundation.org/resource/winterreise-texts-and-translations.
2 Ibid., song no. 18: 'The Stormy Morning'.
3 Bertolt Brecht, 'The Flower Garden' (from *Buckow Elegies*), in *Poems*, London: Methuen, 1976, p. 439.

Winter Garden

1 Roland Barthes, *Camera Lucida*, London: Vintage, 2000, p. 99.

136

2 Ibid., p. 71.

3 Ibid., p. 70.

4 Robert Schumann, 'Melancholy', from *Spanisches Liederspiel*, poetry by Emanuel Geibel, transl. Emily Ezurst, available at https://oxfordsong.org/song/melancholie.

5 Transl. note: 'At-*tune*' translates 'be-*stimmen*', an allusion to Heidegger's notion of fundamental moods, 'Stimmungen', which determine the being of Dasein prior to any particular experience.

Time of the Other

1 Immanuel Kant, *Critique of Pure Reason*, Cambridge: Cambridge University Press, 1998, p. 143.

2 Transl. note: The German 'Anbau' has two meanings, 'cultivation' and 'extension' (especially to a building). As Kant, in this passage, is discussing the 'ampliative principles' – 'Erweiterungs-Grundsätze' – a priori of pure reason, he probably had the second of these meanings in mind.

3 Immanuel Kant, *Anthropology from a Pragmatic Point of View*, Cambridge: Cambridge University Press, 2006, p. 155.

4 Max Scheler, 'Love and Knowledge', in *On Feeling, Knowing, and Valuing*, Chicago: University of Chicago Press, 1992, pp. 147–65; here: p. 164.

Back to the Earth

1 Friedrich Hölderlin, *Hyperion, or The Hermit in Greece*, transl. Howard Gaskill, Cambridge: Open Book Publishers, 2019, p. 47.

2 Theodor W. Adorno, 'Schubert (1928)', in *19th-Century Music*, Vol. 29, No. 1 (Summer 2005), pp. 3–14; here: p. 14; transl. modified. Transl. note: The German is 'Vor

Schuberts Musik stürzt die Träne aus dem Auge, ohne erst die Seele zu befragen.'

3 Theodor W. Adorno, *Aesthetic Theory*, London: Continuum, 1997, p. 276.
4 Ibid., p. 126.
5 Martin Heidegger, 'Building Dwelling Thinking', in *Poetry, Language, Thought*, New York: Harper Collins, 2001, pp. 141–59; here: p. 148.
6 Novalis, *Henry of Ofterdingen*, Cambridge: John Owen, 1842, p. 94. Transl. note: A more literal translation of the first stanza's second line would be: 'Is master of the earth'.

Romanticizing the World

1 Novalis, 'Logological Fragments I' (fragment 66), in *Philosophical Writings*, Albany: State University of New York Press, 1997, pp. 47–66; here: p. 60.
2 Novalis, *Henry of Ofterdingen*, p. 26.
3 Transl. note: My translation.
4 Johann Wolfgang von Goethe, *Theory of Colours*, London: John Murray, 1840, §779, pp. 310f.; transl. amended.
5 Ibid., §§780f, p. 311.
6 Ibid., §765, p. 306.

Winter-flowering Cherry

1 Friedrich Hölderlin, 'The Middle of Life', in *Poems and Fragments*, Ann Arbor: University of Michigan Press, 1966, p. 371.
2 Johann Wolfgang Goethe, *The Sorrows of Young Werther*, Boston: Francis A. Niccolls & Company, 1902, p. 96.
3 Transl. note: As opposed to 'ill weeds grow apace' or 'bad weeds grow tall', the German proverb 'Unkraut vergeht nicht' has a positive slant: no one is perfect, but imperfection also helps to endure hardship and mishaps.

Winter Aconites and Witch Hazel
1 From https://www.gaissmayer.de/web/welt/mit-stauden
-gestalten/duft/jahreszeiten/winter.
2 Transl. note: The German name is 'Zaubernuss', literally:
'magic nut'.

White Forsythia
1 Henry David Thoreau, *Walden: A Fully Annotated Edition*,
New Haven: Yale University Press, 2004, p. 299.

Anemones
1 From https://gottfriedbennpoems.com/the-poems; transl.
modified.

Willow Catkins
1 Hölderlin, *Hyperion*, p. 37.
2 Ibid., p. 81.
3 Ibid., p. 16.

Crocuses
1 Heinrich Heine, *Book of Songs*, in *The Poems of Heine*,
London: George Bell and Sons, 1887, pp. 23–195; here:
p. 66.
2 Transl. note: The German 'wuchern' denotes the uncon-
trolled proliferation of plants, especially those considered
weeds. 'Wucher' means 'usury'.

On Happiness
1 Friedrich Schiller, *On Naïve and Sentimental Poetry*, in
Naïve and Sentimental Poetry and On the Sublime, New
York: Frederick Ungar, 1966, pp. 81–190; here: p. 85;
transl. amended.

Beautiful Names

1 Walter Benjamin, 'In the Sun', from *Thought Figures*, in *Selected Writings*, *Vol. 2, Part 2, 1931–1934*, Cambridge, MA: Harvard University Press, 1999, pp. 662–5; here: p. 662.

2 Byung-Chul Han, *Todesarten: Philosophische Untersuchungen zum Tod*, Munich: Wilhelm Fink, 1998, p. 144.

3 Hölderlin, *Hyperion*, p. 49.

4 Friedrich Nietzsche, *On the Genealogy of Morality*, Cambridge: Cambridge University Press, 2007, p. 12.

5 Friedrich Nietzsche, *Unpublished Fragments (Spring 1885– Spring 1886)*, Stanford: Stanford University Press, 2020, p. 379.

6 Ibid.

Victoria Amazonica

1 Walter Benjamin, *The Arcades Project*, Cambridge, MA: Harvard University Press, 1999, p. 207; transl. modified.

2 Martin Heidegger, *On the Way to Language*, New York: Harper & Row, 1971, p. 16; transl. amended.

3 The etymology is not certain, but Early New High German has 'ungezibere', meaning 'impure animal', i.e. possibly animals 'not suitable for sacrifice'. And Old High German 'zebar' may mean 'sacrifice'. See *Kluge: Etymologisches Wörterbuch* (25th edition), Berlin: De Gruyter, 2011, p. 942.

Autumn Crocuses

1 Hölderlin, *Hyperion*, p. 45; transl. modified.

2 Wilhelm Müller, 'Letzte Hoffnung', from Franz Schubert, *Winterreise*, available at https://hampsongfoundation.org /resource/winterreise-texts-and-translations/#letzte-hoff nung.

3 Hölderlin, *Hyperion*, p. 21.

1 https://www.google.com/search?q=georges+moustaki+il +y+avait+un+jardin+lyrics&rlz=1C1KMZB_enGB586G B586&oq=moustaki+ily+a&aqs=chrome.2.69i57j46i13i 512j0i22i3017.6641j0j4&sourceid=chrome&ie=UTF-8; transl. modified.

2 Transl. note: The translation follows the German. The section on 'Agnos' in Dioscorides, *De Materia Medica*, Johannesburg: Ibidis Press, 2000, pp. 137f., differs significantly.

3 Byung-Chul Han, *Absence: On the Culture and Philosophy of the Far East*, Cambridge: Polity, 2023, pp. 39f.

4 Franz Schubert, 'The Phantom Suns', from *Winterreise*. Quoted after Hampsong Foundation, transl. William Mann, available at https://hampsongfoundation.org/ resource/winterreise-texts-and-translations.

5 Transl. note: The German for 'forget-me-not' is 'Männertreu', literally 'men's faithfulness'. The German sentence 'Männertreu blüht besonders treu' plays on this: 'Men's faithfulness flowers especially faithfully', that is, reliably.

6 Jean Baudrillard, *Seduction*, Montreal: New World Perspectives, 2001, p. 100.

7 Robert N. Huey, 'Journal of My Father's Last Days. Issa's Chichi no Shūen Nikki', *Monumenta Nipponica*, Vol. 39, No. 1 (1984), pp. 25–54; here: p. 49.

8 Theodor W. Adorno, 'Notiz über Namen' (Note on names), in *Gesammelte Werke*, Vol. 20.2 (Aesthetica, Miscellanea), Frankfurt am Main: Suhrkamp, 1997, p. 533f; here: p. 534. Transl. note: The full passage runs: 'If the lines of our fate become entangled and form an inextricable net, then names are again and again the seals that are imprinted on the lineages; they protect the lineages against us seizing hold of them, and us from getting

entangled in them, by setting before us initials that we do not understand but obey.'

9 Matsuo Bashô, *The Essential Bashô*, Boston: Shambhala, 1999, p. 119.
10 Rainer Maria Rilke, *Die Gedichte*, Frankfurt am Main: Insel, 2006, p. 835, p. 613, and p. 478.
11 Martin Heidegger, 'Letter on "Humanism"', in *Pathmarks*, Cambridge: Cambridge University Press, 1998, pp. 239–76; here: p. 243.
12 Hölderlin, *Hyperion*, p. 8.
13 Rainer Maria Rilke, *Duino Elegies*, in *Duino Elegies and The Sonnets to Orpheus*, Boston: Houghton Mifflin, 1975, p. 5.
14 Transl. note: 'will *rule supreme* again' translates 'wird wieder *walten*', an allusion to Walter Benjamin's 'Critique of Violence' (in *Selected Writings, Vol. 1: 1913–1926*, Cambridge, MA: Harvard University Press, 2004, pp. 236–52), which ends by suggesting that divine violence – as opposed to 'mythic' and 'executive' violence – might be called 'die waltende' (Walter Benjamin, *Gesammelte Schriften*, Vol. II.1, Frankfurt am Main: Suhrkamp, 1991, p. 203).
15 Transl. note: The German word for 'organ' is 'Orgel'; it sounds very similar to '(H)orugel'.
16 Transl. note: My translation. I consulted the translation on the following website, which also gives the original Italian: https://paralleltexts.blog/2016/09/16/la-piog gia-nel-pinetorain-in-the-pine-forest-by-gabriele-dan nunzio.
17 Transl. note: The German verbs form a minimal pair: 'hineingeboren' and 'hineingeborgen'.
18 Hildegard Geisberger, *Platon 'Symposion'* (June 2011), pp. 17f., available at https://eh-geisberger.de/dokumente /Vortrag_Platon_Symposion.pdf.

19 Transl. note: 'Staudenmarkt', literally 'market for perennial plants'. See 'https://Berliner Staudenmarkt.de.

20 Martin Heidegger, 'The Thinker as Poet', in *Poetry, Language, Thought*, pp. 2–14; here: p. 14. Transl. note: 'Mist diffuses' translates 'Regen rinnt', more literally 'rain trickles'.

21 Friedrich Hölderlin, 'Patmos', in *Hymns and Fragments*, Princeton: Princeton University Press, 1984, pp. 89–101; here: p. 89; transl. modified.